Developing Leadership in the Teaching Church

**CHICAGO BLACK METHODISTS
FOR CHURCH RENEWAL**
212 EAST 95th ST.
CHICAGO, ILLINOIS 60619

Developing Leadership in the Teaching Church

Jan Chartier

Judson Press ® Valley Forge

DEVELOPING LEADERSHIP IN THE TEACHING CHURCH
Copyright © 1985
Judson Press, Valley Forge, PA 19482-0851

All rights reserved. No part of this publication may be reproduced, stored in a retrieval system, or transmitted in any form or by any means, electronic, mechanical, photocopying, recording, or otherwise, without the prior permission of the copyright owner, except for brief quotations included in a review of the book.

Library of Congress Cataloging in Publication Data

Chartier, Jan.
  Developing leadership in the teaching church.

  1. Christian leadership. I. Title.
BV652.1.C5 1985   262   85-31
ISBN 0-8170-1067-X

The name JUDSON PRESS is registered as a trademark in the U.S. Patent Office. Printed in the U.S.A.

Dedicated to the memory of
my parents, Fred and Lelia Duncan, who practiced
quality leadership in many areas of life
and who gave to me the gift of
two different but effective leadership approaches
to learn from and to follow.

Foreword

There are those who would say, and strongly so, that no issue so dramatically and urgently confronts the church today as that of leadership, be it volunteer or professional.

We are concerned here, however, with volunteer leaders. This significant group of persons is the primary source of leadership for the structural and programmatic activity of the church. Today, however, we are faced with the reality that the potential leadership available to the church is not as large, as available, or as willing as the leadership of another era. The reasons are numerous. Neither the dilemma nor the solutions are simple:

- The volunteers of the 1940s and 1950s have reached the point where they want to pass on the leadership roles for church and community. "We have done our share," is the feeling expressed.
- The decades of the 1960s and 1970s did not create a new cadre of leaders ready to assume automatically the tasks of their predecessors. Those coming forward were a new type of leader with broader interests, a greater sense of intentionality, and a desire to know personally why they were involved. They tend to be selective and intentional in their leadership actions.

- The environment for leadership has changed. The availability of persons has diminished. Economic needs often dictate that both parents be employed outside the home; single-parent families have grown in number; vocational pressures are of greater intensity; the number of organizations seeking volunteer leadership has multiplied significantly.

The end result of these and other factors has given rise to a new seriousness on the part of the church in its concern for the motivation and support of leadership.

In *Developing Leadership in the Teaching Church* Dr. Chartier provides an indication of and a response to that mood of seriousness. It is both foundational and practical. Some would say philosophical, rather than foundational. But I choose the latter because Dr. Chartier involves herself in providing a base for the more practical aspects of leadership. We might refer to these as the "how to's" or the methods and approaches to day-by-day functioning of leaders. In this realm attention is given to:

—the creation of a climate for effective leadership,
—the understanding of the varieties of leadership style and the interaction of styles with group needs,
—the necessary qualities of effective leadership,
—the nature of support by and for leadership.

The practical is always welcome! But it is of little value without foundation. Our grasp of the importance of a qualitative leadership that is birthed out of biblical and theological understandings is essential. Dr. Chartier cites the importance of knowing why we are about *what* we are when she says, "If we are to become involved in the church's leadership processes then we must have our formative, controlling principles based solidly in our biblical/theological foundation. We as Christians are not free to follow any voice or adopt any theory because it is attractive and appears to work. If it does things such as manipulate human beings, thwart the dignity of human personhood, add to the burden of the oppressed or increase the deprivation of the poor, then it does not belong to God's people. We must search out a better way."

Developing Leadership in the Teaching Church has been written as one step in aiding our understanding of the concept of the teaching church. The teaching church is described through the identification of five functions as the essence of the teaching church. "Developing leaders for a variety of ministries" is one of the five functions. The other four are:

Affirming the foundations of the teaching ministry;
Planning for the most effective teaching ministry;
Nurturing persons in Christian growth;
Enabling the fulfillment of the church's mission in the world.

Developing Leadership in the Teaching Church will be followed by books on the other four functions. The next to appear will be a book on "affirming the foundations of the teaching ministry."

It is said that "to describe Christian community as the teaching church is to catch the true essence of the church and to affirm the centrality of its teaching ministry."[1] Dr. Chartier enhances our understanding of the teaching church generally and the issue of leadership development specifically in this writing effort.

So now we have in hand a book that draws our attention to an issue—leadership! What to do with such a resource is an appropriate question. Fortunately, Dr. Chartier, able teacher that she is, provides in the appendix of the book a set of session plans, eight to be exact, that will enable the use of this book as a text for study groups.

Beneficiaries of such a study experience would include those responsible for leader development in any congregation, so committees and boards of Christian education will benefit from in-depth study. The broader use could also well include the congregation as a whole, either through special study groups, in an all-church retreat using the book and its study guide as the program, or in the standing organizations of the church such as boards and committees.

Many things have changed in the church over the centuries. But the need for leadership has remained constant. This day, more than any other, calls for consistent and continual attention to leadership development. In *Developing Leadership in the Teaching Church* there is thoughtful direction and an opportunity for intentional action.

John L. Carroll
Director of Division of Church Education
American Baptist Churches in the U.S.A.

[1] "The Teaching Church," Grant W. Hanson, *Baptist Leader,* September, 1977.

Contents

Chapters

1 Looking at Church Leadership	13
2 Biblical Touchstones for Church Leadership	19
3 Spiritual Gifts and Church Leadership	29
4 Lifelong Pilgrims in Church Leadership	41
5 Creating a Climate for Church Leadership Commitment	51
6 Church Leadership in Action	63
7 Keys to Effective Church Leadership	71
8 Responding Supportively to Church Leadership	81
A Final Challenge	95

Appendixes

1 Brief Session Outlines for a Group Studying This Book	97
2 Suggestions for Planning Leadership Dedication and Recognition Services	103
3 Resources for Training and Reading	107
Notes	111

1
CHAPTER

Looking at Church Leadership

Social organizations have a basic need for quality leaders. The church is no exception! Leaders are important key persons. They help to create a dream and a vision toward which a group can move. They establish a climate and tone among the members which call the organization to mobilize its energies and to take bold action to make the dream happen. They enlist the help of all those who would be a part of what the group is to be now and in the future. They allow the group members freedom to move forward at their own pace and in their own style, but they consistently set forth the challenge to keep moving toward the dream and to contribute to making the vision happen. Good leaders in the church will help members achieve their goals.

When a social organization is lacking competent leaders, it eventually begins to drift and flounder. The church is no exception! Leaders are vital to its identity formation, its inner well-being, and its outward performance.

When a fresh vitality emerges in the life of a church, it can often be traced to a core of leaders who have not been willing to settle for mediocre quality, but who have determined to devote their energies in helping church members catch a vision of becoming something more.

The ideas in this book grow from the deep conviction that leadership is a critical factor related to how well the church is doing in reaching its goal to be God's people involved in God's mission in the world. The church is never without leadership, but the vitality and kind of leadership vary from time to time. To be effective in accomplishing its mission, the church needs quality leadership in all arenas of its life.

Called to Quality Leadership

All of us as believers are called to make certain that quality leadership happens in our church. None of us can shift our responsibility to others. We must be sure that we are doing all we can to help the church be an authentic witness to our Lord by its words and ways of living.

We may understand our responsibility for quality leadership more clearly if we consider the difference between "leaders" and "leadership."

Leaders

Leaders are specific persons. Groups and organizations usually have leaders who are selected to fill certain positions. These persons are sometimes referred to as formal leaders. In the church the pastor is a leader; the moderator is a leader; the persons who chair boards or committees are leaders. Sometimes leaders are elected to their positions for a specific term of office; other leaders hold their positions for an unlimited period of time. Leaders may have job descriptions to guide them in knowing what is expected of them. Usually these expectations are, or at least can be, made available to all members of the congregation so that everyone knows what that person is supposed to be doing. Formal leaders are important to the well-being of the church.

Being an elected, formal leader is a positive challenge to some church members. Such people enjoy these kinds of opportunities to serve. They view their position as a leader as a special place where they belong and where they can serve in the ministry of the church. Others, for a variety of reasons, shy away from such involvements. They make it known that they do not want to be leaders. They find the responsibility too burdensome and overwhelming. It seems obvious that the first persons are called to be leaders. The second group seems not to share in that calling.

However, in analyzing what happens in a group, there are likely to be some surprises. There are usually persons in addition to the named, formal leaders who influence and direct what happens in the group. They may not think of themselves as leaders at all; yet they may in fact have as much or in some cases even more power than the formal leaders. Even though they don't think of themselves that way, these persons are leaders, too. They may lack formal titles and job descriptions, but they shape the identity of the group and direction in which it is moving. These persons are sometimes called informal leaders. It is difficult to know how informal leaders have come to their position in the group. They simply seem to emerge. If asked how they became informal group leaders, they may be puzzled. They are likely not to think of themselves as leaders at all. They may even declare that they have no intention of influencing the group. In some cases they may not be aware of their power to change the group's direction.

Churches have both formal and informal leaders. Constitutions, organizational charts, and job descriptions tend to give the impression that formal leaders are the ones who have the opportunities to shape the life of the congregation. In reality, much of what happens in congregational life may be designed by those who are informal leaders. It is a healthy situation when the leaders, formal and informal, work together as a team striving to accomplish agreed-upon goals.

Leadership

Leadership is a more abstract idea. Our son recently came home with the "Leadership Award" from summer soccer camp. I asked him what it meant. He began to respond in very general terms. He hadn't explained much when he shrugged his shoulders and said, "I guess it's pretty hard to pin down in words. Everybody just kind of knows what it is. It just happens."

Leadership is like that. It is present and operative in groups, but when we try to reduce it to words, it becomes vague and illusive.

16 DEVELOPING LEADERSHIP IN THE TEACHING CHURCH

Leadership has to do with all of the things that are done in a group or organization to move it in certain directions.

Leadership happens in the interactions among the group members. Martin Buber talked about the I-Thou relationship.[1] He emphasized the importance of the hyphen in the term, or the "betweenness." We don't see it, but we know it is there. We recognize its importance. Somehow we sense the relational hyphen. We know that our own well-being is knit to the well-being of another.

Leadership is like the relational hyphen. Perhaps that is one reason why it is so difficult to pin down. It is larger than one person and even larger than the sum of all the individuals who belong to the group. Rather, it is molded and shaped through the many ways all the members come together and interact to get things done.

Leadership includes outstanding things people do, such as making speeches, chairing meetings, keeping records; but it also encompasses the inconspicuous things, such as being on time, seconding a motion, joining in prayer, signing up for a work project. Leadership does not belong exclusively to the formal and informal leaders; it belongs to all the members of the church. Everyone who participates as a member of the church shares in the leadership responsibility.

Leaders and followers must work in a team relationship if leadership is to be healthy and accomplish important things. Being a leader implies that one has some followers. Leaders by definition influence what happens in the life of a group; however, influence works only if there are sufficient members who choose to move in the direction pointed by the leader.

Leaders are easily thwarted if no one follows their leading. Leaders can have the most brilliant of ideas and carefully formulated plans; but without other group members working alongside, the ideas and plans are impotent. Such schemes accomplish nothing except perhaps to demonstrate the potential of the leaders who proposed them. We acknowledge these kinds of situations with statements like, "It's too bad no one had time to get involved in her project. It was a great idea" or, "He lost his following. One by one the people dropped out until no one was left."

Two concrete examples may help us visualize how shared leadership does make a difference in the outcome of what happens in the life of the church. One leader proposes what seems to be a good plan for the church. A few of the other members point out some factors that need to be considered: "The members of the congregation tend to be very busy in their jobs at the time of year the plan is to start." "There are already two important projects under way which will not be completed." "A similar plan has been talked about in another committee. Maybe we should have some conversation with them and look at their plans." As these and other factors are discussed, the plan is modified. The timing is changed so that the starting date comes at a more opportune season. The plan is to be done one step at a time as the people and financial resources are available. Members of the other committee have become involved. Ownership and commitment are high. The plan won't happen as early nor as fast, but it will get under way and the chances for completion are good. Quality leadership has been shared.

In another congregation a church leader proposes a plan. There is little discussion to provide feedback for the group. A vote is taken. It is positive. However, members leave the meeting wondering if others have as many questions as they do about whether the group has made the best decision. The leader's plan has been recorded in the minutes. When the time comes to begin implementation, only a "faithful few" are present to invest energy in getting the job done. The project limps along. As reports come back to the group, guilt and discouragement settle in. The leader feels betrayed; the group members feel like dismal failures. Leadership in this church has stumbled and fallen apart.

You can probably add the specific details to these two illustrations from your own experiences in the life of the churches with which you are familiar. Variations of these examples are common happenings in church life. Some churches seem to have quality leadership experiences most of the time; others rarely do. Many churches have a mix of some good and some not so good.

Whether the quality of the leadership in the church can be improved is often given little consideration in the church. The assumption sometimes seems to be that given a particular leader in a specific group, leadership was destined to function the way it did. There wasn't much anyone could do to change it.

Leadership Improvement

An encouraging word comes to us from behavioral science research. People can learn to be more effective in contributing to quality leadership in the groups where they belong. There are understandings, attitudes, and, particularly, skills which both leaders and followers can acquire to assure that leadership will function more effectively in their group. All members of the group can improve the ways in which they share leadership among themselves. We do not have to settle for things as they are. We must set a goal for becoming the best group members we can be. Sometimes we may be leaders; sometimes followers. Always the challenge is to recognize that leadership responsibility belongs to each of us individually and to all of us together.

Persons who think of themselves primarily as insignificant, unimportant members of the church may need to be encouraged to reconsider their view. If quality leadership is to happen, every group member is important.

Recently an incident in the life of a friend caused me to take a new look at the importance of all group members. My friend had minor foot surgery in which a section of his little toe was removed, and other adjustments were made to correct some emerging problems with his foot. After the surgery my friend was assisted from the doctor's office to the car and driven home. The next day, when he stood to walk, he found that his equilibrium was unsettled. His sense of balance was ajar. That seemingly insignificant, unimportant part of his body had been doing its job for years. Now it was gone and major adjustment had to be made.

This book has been written with the hope that all of us will do some reflecting and rethinking about church leadership. We are all called to leadership responsibility. Even those of us who may consider ourselves "little toes" have an important place in making quality leadership happen. We are God's people with a great task to do. It is imperative that we work together in a leadership team committed that the ministry of our Lord will be done through us in first rate ways.

2
CHAPTER

Biblical Touchstones for Church Leadership

It is in the pages of Scripture that we discover God's revealed messages for the people of God today. These messages are not always obvious upon first reading. We have to become serious students of the Bible who diligently study, who employ rigorous principles of interpretation, and who pray for discernment under the guidance of the Holy Spirit.[1]

A deep personal conviction of mine is that Christian people everywhere must commit themselves to study of the Bible, to prayer, and to careful theological formulation. Through these endeavors we gain clarity as to who we are called to be and how we are to behave. Our certainty about our identity as God's people begins to increase. We gain confidence about living as a people of love and justice in a world which prefers not to be hassled with principles that call for radical change. Our theological formulations, firm and solid, yet open to refinement and new insights into God's truth, become the foundation from which we launch out to become whom we are called to be in this world.

If we are to become involved in the church's leadership processes, then we must have our formative, controlling principles based solidly in our biblical/theological foundation. We as Christians are not free to follow any voice or adopt any theory simply because it is attractive and appears to work. If it does things such as manipulate human beings, thwart the dignity of human personhood, add to the burden of the oppressed, or increase the deprivation of the poor, then it does not belong to God's people. We must search out a better way.

The purpose of this chapter is to lift up some biblical touchstones which help us clarify what leadership processes in the church ought to look like and accomplish. Touchstones for me are theological areas which seem to hold great potential as we study and gain understanding for informing us who we are or should be as a Christian community trying to live faithfully as God's people. Touchstones are there for us to come back to again and again to be reminded of truths we have lost sight of, or perhaps to see something for the first time because we are now ready to understand. We initially shove off into ministry and service from our touchstones, trying to incorporate into our way of being what we have learned. We return to dialogue with one another in the presence of our touchstones, bringing our experiences with us. When we are renewed, we move into ministry again. It is an ongoing process for the Christian community. The task is a continuing one.

This chapter contains what for me are foundational biblical touchstones. I hope you choose to study these in greater depth and even add touchstones which seem particularly relevant to you. This presentation simply points a direction. It is a starting point.

Jesus: The Person and the Work

The central touchstone for Christians is the life and ministry of our Lord. His redemptive work calls us into being and provides us a way. He is the New Covenant with humanity. It is in him that we live and move and have our being. By seeing him, we see something of the Creator-Redeemer God. We learn who we are supposed to be as God's children. Let's consider some of the understandings we gain by learning about Jesus and leadership.

Jesus began his ministry with baptism. At that time he was anointed with the Holy Spirit. He went to the desert, where for forty days he struggled with Satan and the forces of evil. Victorious, he returned filled with the power of the Spirit and moved directly into an intensive ministry. He continued to be a person of learning and prayer. The Old Testament Scriptures were important to him; he had a pattern of drawing aside for prayer. He was committed to obedience to God's will and way.

Christians involved in leadership, like Jesus, must be seekers hungry for biblical truth. We must be people of prayer. We must be obedient to God's will and way as they are revealed to us.

Jesus was prophetic in his ministry. He was familiar with the religious leaders of the day and with their ways of adding to the burdens of the people with laws upon laws, making the living God seem more and more punitive, remote, and inaccessible. The words of the faith community had become hollow, filled with a pious ring but with little or no integrity. There was a great gulf between the truths which were lifted up as ideals and the injustices which were practiced in day-to-day living. They were a people of empty, misled faith.

Jesus' words to these people were direct and clear, condemning them for having lost the way of the God they professed to serve. Repeatedly he challenged their assumptions, often by interacting with the marginal persons in ways which turned the accepted piousness upside down. Jesus was a prophet in word and action. His lifestyle showed that God's way was far from what the people were being asked to believe by the religious leaders. Jesus frequently moved into a confrontation where he spoke and acted as a prophet. His prophetic ministry was a large factor in directing his pathway to the cross.

Our world needs prophetic persons speaking God's message. We need leaders who will confront the hollow, unjust, uncaring ways in which people shape their personal lives and by which they structure their societies. The sinful ways which permeate our living, leading to alienation and brokenness, need to be challenged. It is beyond question that there is an urgency about finding prophets who can call our global community to faithfulness.

There are some cautions to be raised. Jesus is our incarnate Lord. His message from God and his authentic ways of living lie beyond our humanity. Our prophetic undertakings must not trap us into believing that we as human creatures have a corner on God's truth. Today's prophets must speak confrontational challenges to the ways of living and the structures of society which perpetuate brokenness. At the same time they must be open to recognize where their own messages have been vulnerable to partial truths and distortions. Such a balance is difficult to achieve and maintain.

It seems to be crucial that the Christian community follow through on a responsibility to nurture and support its leaders, whose call is to prophetic ministry. Such a faithful undergirding position may seem almost impossible when the words of confrontation are turned toward the church itself. Yet the task is necessary if prophets are to have a resourceful, supportive home base and a community which enters into dialogues of accountability to faithful interpretations of God's Word.

Perhaps the most unexpected aspect of Jesus' approach to life and ministry was his servanthood. The anticipated Messiah was to be a person of grandeur, a royal leader coming in power and glory. The Messiah was to overthrow all the unjust nations and establish a new rulership. Everyone would recognize the coming One. The glory, the power, the majesty would be so sensational that no one could miss or mistake such a person.

But who was this Jesus whom some called the Messiah? His parents were humble people from Galilee. He learned carpentry from his father. He roamed about the countryside with fishermen, tax collectors, and other common folk. He reached out to the "no-counts" in life. He healed those who were sick, gave sight to those without vision, set free those whose lives had been captive to sin and brokenness.

Who was this Jesus whose life was one of servanthood, bringing good news to the world's downtrodden? Some of those who met Jesus were able to turn away from the predominant expectations and call Jesus "Lord," "Messiah," "the Christ," "Master." The blockages were too high and too deep for others. They simply would not choose to change. They saw Jesus as the deluded, evil one who deserved to die a murderer's death on a cross. Our responses to Jesus as a servant may be similar to those of centuries ago. Some of us will capture the vision of what it means to be a servant leader binding up the wounds of the world's downtrodden, maintaining a stance of building feelings of preciousness and worth so people can choose life for themselves. Others of us will find the blockages to becoming servant leaders very high and deep. We believe so much in success and prestige according to the world's terms that it will seem like an insurmountable task to think in servant leader terms.

Jesus was obedient to God's will. He was both a prophet and a servant. We are similarly called to obedience. Some of us will have gifts to speak and live prophetically; others will move into the world as servants healing, binding, and loving—at every turn reaching out with compassion. A few of us may be called to be both prophets and servants. Whatever our calling, we must respond in consistent faithfulness.

The People of God

In the Old Testament we discover that Israel is frequently called the people of God. They were a people specially chosen by God for a unique purpose. They were chosen to be a light to all the nations that those people, too, might come to know the living God. Israel was to live in such a way that it would be an instrument to show what living according to God's will and intention means. Their way of being a people was to demonstrate God's covenantal love, righteousness, and justice.

But this chosen nation had a hard time being faithful to its task. Israel turned from a covenantal trust walk with God to political alliances, financial intrigues, and the acceptance of foreign gods. Internally the people of Israel did not live righteously with one another. The wealthy used their power to further increase their riches at the expense of the poor. Their faith became more a matter of hollow ritual than a true worship and service of their redeemer God.

Through the long historical pilgrimage of Israel's in-and-out faith walk with God there is a fascinating and illuminating leadership dynamic. Outstanding leaders were raised up at strategic junctures when the people most needed to be led back to God's way. The criteria seemed to be that these leaders were to be obedient to God; they were to lead the people to forsake their waywardness; they were to call them to remembrance of their identity and purpose. The possible list of names of such persons would be long. It would include the patriarchs, the judges, the kings, the prophets, and others. Some of them would be familiar, like Moses, Joshua, Esther, Saul,

David, and Solomon. Others would be obscure and unfamiliar. They all appeared at times of pronounced need.

Their leadership often emerged because of a call from God. Moses encountered God in a burning-bush incident. It was Samuel, a prophet with the Lord's message, who called Saul to become king. Jeremiah's call came in relationship to the movement of an almond branch. Isaiah met the Lord in the temple. There are no details given about the many ways in which God called some of the leaders to their positions, but the call seemed to be important to them. The belief that God was working through them kept these leaders moving forward through formidable barriers when it would have been easy and sometimes safer to give up.

Israel was expected to be true to the covenant which God had established in the beginning. They were to be God's people, living according to God's ways. Unfortunately it didn't always happen. Even the best rulers had their moments of unrighteous living. King David was later idealized by the people and known as the greatest of kings; yet is was he who arranged for the murder of Uriah; who committed adultery with Bathsheba; whose own family was in shambles as he grew older. The prophet Nathan was God's spokesprophet to David. He called for King David's repentance and a turning back to God's ways.

What can we learn from the experiences of the people of God about leadership in our own day? Even as the people of Israel needed leaders to help them be faithful to the covenant and its righteous ways of living, so the church needs leaders who will call the church to its identity as God's people with a mission to the whole world. Our primary purpose as Christian leaders is to serve God and the church. That should be our motive and our goal.

Just because we are leaders, there is no guarantee that we will continue in a faithful walk in God's ways. We must learn to hold each other accountable. We cannot rest on the assumption that "because leaders say it, then it is all right, and true to God's ways." Leaders are vulnerable to human error and sin. Perhaps even more so because they carry a heavy load on behalf of so many. Over time they can lose perspective. We need to hear prophetic voices among us and consider their messages. All of us must work together to discern whether we as a church are moving in a direction that God would have us go.

The call from God was important to the leaders of Israel. God's call continues to operate in peoples' lives today—sometimes dramatically, sometimes subtly. We may resist the call just as they did. We need to develop a faith community climate which allows us the freedom to explore the many ways in which God is calling us and how we can respond to God's call.

We can learn from Israel that changes in leadership can be times when God's Word is spoken in fresh new ways which bring new life and energy among the people. That happens when the new leaders are truly committed to God's ways and are being led by the Spirit to accomplish this task. Some of Israel's kings lasted three months or less! They were corrupt before taking office. There is no guarantee that a new leader will be Spirit-led. There is a lesson to be learned in using discrimination when selecting leaders.

The Body of Christ

One of the primary images used by the apostle Paul in describing the church is the body of Christ. The head of the body is Christ. All those who have faith in him are part of the body. There are many diverse members, but the diversity is not divisive in nature. In fact the diversity can be used to contribute to the well-being of the whole. The eye needs the hand, and the head needs the feet. We cannot say, "We don't need each other." Our well-being depends upon all the parts of the body working together.

Divisions are to be abhorred. They destroy rather than build up the body. In Christ, old divisions which have kept people apart are now broken down. We are all God's children together, part of the body of Christ. There is no Jew or Gentile, no slave or free persons, no male or female, for all are one. (See Galatians 3:28). Faith in Christ invalidates any definitions that once made one person superior to another for any reason. The body is not composed of unequals, but of persons whose faith makes them one in Christ. Love of one another, regardless of our differences, must mark everything the church is and does if it is to be the body of Christ. It must be the love of Christ which binds and controls us.

The concept of the church as the body helps us understand some important aspects of leadership and being leaders. Leadership belongs to the whole church. Everyone who is part of the body is responsible for its well-being. Those who serve as leaders are not better as human beings, nor do they have greater worth in the sight of God, nor have they done a superb job of living by the law. Rather, they are faithful servants of Christ, along with other members of the body. They may have a special job to do for a time, but the purpose is that all members of the body might show love to one another and to the world.

Any leadership dynamics which create divisions or nurture a climate where one group becomes an elite subgroup are to be held suspect. Everything that is done is not to set apart an elite, in human terms, but to build up the whole body for the glory of God. Some churches have found themselves paralyzed because of conflicts among leaders and their respective subgroups. These divisions weaken the body and distort its witness. We must work to identify, explore, and understand our differences to the extent that all of our gifts can bring glory to God's purposes.

Because old divisions which elevated the worth of some persons over another have been broken down, then all persons are eligible candidates to serve as leaders when the time is right and their gifts are needed. For years in predominantly white denominations in the United States, white males were the accepted leaders. They established policy and set direction. Persons of ethnic minority backgrounds and women were involved only in restricted ways and rarely where they had much power. That situation is changing, but we have a long way to go before we have insight and grace enough among ourselves to select our leaders because they are God's persons with the gifts needed for that moment.

The Holy Spirit

In both the Old and the New Testament the Spirit is seen as crucial in the life of the people of faith. In the Old Testament God is active in history and in the lives of persons through the Spirit. When the Spirit moves in history, God's presence is made known in action. God's Spirit touched the lives of persons in very real ways literally to give them life and power or illness and torment. (See 1 Samuel 16:13-14.)

God's Spirit became present in a new way in the life of our Lord. The Spirit filled his life at baptism and empowered his ministry. It was Jesus who promised that when he returned to be with God, the Spirit would come among his followers in a new way. The Spirit would guide them into truth.

As Jesus had promised, the Spirit was given to his followers (See John 21:22-23; Acts 2.) Through the Spirit, many things could be done by the church to carry on Christ's ministry. The Spirit finds its dwelling place in the body of Christ. The church is the Spirit's temple. The Spirit abides among the believers to bind together, to teach, to guide, to comfort, to enlighten, to empower, to challenge, and to convict. When the Spirit truly abides among the people of God, they experience unity and power. They go forth in the name of Christ to witness to the living God's presence and action in history.

If we come to this touchstone for insight and guidance into today's leadership, we are immediately impressed that the presence of the Spirit is crucial. Christ continues to indwell us through the Spirit. When the church thinks of leadership, the entire process must be submitted to the guidance of the Spirit. As a people—leaders and followers—we must open ourselves to a more abundant indwelling of the Spirit that we might experience more fully the leading and empowering which have been promised to us. We must claim the promise for our own that our ministries may be full.

The Last Days

History in the Bible moves toward an end point that has not yet happened. The early church expected the return of Christ at any moment. People knew that the final days when God's reign would be complete marked the time when God's intentions would be fully worked out. History as known would end. Eternity would begin. In the meantime, many things had been started but not finished. It was an in-between period, during which they would continue to struggle with the powers of sin and evil. They would know persecution. While they waited, they were to be alert, ever watchful for temptation and sin. They were to be faithful and obedient in worship and service. They could not totally escape sin and its effects, nor could they know what it meant to live fully in Christ's way. They had to study and grow in the Christian life. They had to learn to walk in the Spirit and move away from ways of living that would lead to brokenness.

We continue to wait for the last days. As we look at the overwhelming global problems that surround us, we may believe that God will soon act to bring history to a close, but we do not know that. Only God knows the time. So our leadership must take into account the between-time in which we live. We, too, will struggle with sin and evil. We must be alert to temptation. We must be faithful in worship and learning. We must be obedient in our mission.

Some Summary Words

There is much we can learn about leadership from many sources, but as Christians our foundations need to be in God's Word. Painstaking study and appropriation of our understandings are key for us. Five biblical touchstones have been raised—Jesus: The Person and the Work; The People of God; The Body of Christ; The Holy Spirit; and The Last Days. Much more could be written about each one. This chapter points directions for further study which will be crucial if our touchstones are to deepen.

3
CHAPTER

Spiritual Gifts and Church Leadership

Leadership in the church as the body of Christ and spiritual gifts are inseparably intertwined at many points. If one is to explore adequately the meaning of leadership in the church, then it is necessary to consider the meaning and significance of spiritual gifts. How well any church accomplishes its mission is linked to how qualitatively the spiritual gifts present in that congregation are used.

Let's move into this chapter by doing some imagining. I call it "turning the clock back," when through the visualizing power of our minds we try to think what it would have been like to have lived through a historical event centuries ago. In this case we will go back to a time shortly following the resurrection of Jesus, after he had ascended to be in God's presence. You may want to read Acts 2 as background.

START IMAGINING. We are in the city of Jerusalem. The city is very crowded. No one seems to notice us. We fit right in with the other out-of-town visitors. Before long we join the followers of Jesus who believe that Jesus is God's Son and whose lives have been changed. We are all in one house. It is a difficult time for us. Jesus has gone and we need him. We believe in him, but we are uncertain about the future. We know that he told us that we must go into the whole world to tell others about him, to baptize them and to teach them his way. But without Jesus it all seems very difficult. Our plans seem so feeble. There are real dangers and risks. There is no doubt many of us will be persecuted. Our very lives may be at stake. How are we going to do it? Even those who knew Jesus best seem discouraged. We spend time praying, hoping that an answer will come. We wait—and wait—and wait!

A strange silence fills the room. Suddenly an unfamiliar sound, like the rush of a tornado, bursts in. Then we see an unexplainable sight, like tiny flames of fire resting on each person. And we know the Spirit has come, just as Jesus promised.

Some begin to speak in foreign languages. Spectators who had heard the strange sound come to look. They recognize their own languages being spoken by common folk from Galilee. They are amazed. In their own ways all of Jesus' followers are telling about God's mighty acts—the greatest being the resurrection of Jesus. Some of the onlookers begin to make accusations such as "they're drunk" or "they're crazy."

After a time, Peter stands up and begins to explain to them that this has been the outpouring of the Spirit. He tells them about Jesus, the Christ, our Lord. When they ask how they, too, can follow Jesus, Peter tells them, "Repent, be baptized, and become a part of us." Many of them now decide to become part of us. They want to join our fellowship; they want to learn to pray; they are eager to study; they want to share in our breaking of bread. Our numbers are growing. The Spirit is doing amazing and wonderful things among us. We are all able to speak the Word of God with boldness. We are filled with the Spirit. We are even amazing ourselves. *STOP IMAGINING.*

Today we continue to celebrate this momentous event in the life of the church. Many Jews had gathered in Jerusalem because of the Hebrew festival of Pentecost. It was one of the harvest celebrations when they also remembered the giving of the Law at Sinai. It was an appropriate time for the coming of the Holy Spirit to the disciples so that many could witness the marvelous happenings. It provided a harvest climate for the new church.

The Christians began to move out with boldness to tell of salvation through Jesus. Immediately there was a negative reaction from the Jewish priests and other authorities. The scene was set for a continuing battle. Read Acts, chapters 3 and 4, to get a feel for how this happened. You might learn a great deal by "turning the clock back" again, only this time try to imagine yourself as a loyal Jew trying to react to these "heretical Christians."

The Holy Spirit was God's gift to the church. Through the Spirit came understanding and power to be and do those things which Jesus had set before his followers. The mission of God would not stop because Jesus was no longer living on the earth. It would continue to spread, carried out in the life and ministry of the church, empowered by the Spirit's presence. The Spirit imparted spiritual gifts to the believers so that together they might continue the ministry of Jesus. While individuals are bestowed with the spiritual gifts, it is always important to remember that the gifts are entrusted within the context of the Christian community. They are present for the purpose of service and mission. They are to be used to build the strength of the body so that the whole world eventually hears and comes to believe that we must live according to God's plan. The purpose of this chapter is to gain some insight into the nature of spiritual gifts and how they relate to leadership in the church.

Some Key New Testament Passages

There are four passages in the New Testament which seem to be key when one is trying to focus on the nature of spiritual gifts and why they were given to Christian people. It would be helpful if you were to read the passages as if they were written into this chapter. The following paragraphs will give a brief perspective to help you gain some background.

1. *Romans 12:1-13.* Romans is Paul's letter of introduction to the Roman Christians prior to his arrival among them. In the letter he is explaining the fundamental core of the Christian faith as he sees it. He uses as a theme the righteousness of God. In the early chapters of the letter Paul has discussed how God's righteousness has been revealed, particularly in Jesus Christ. His discussion of spiritual gifts in chapter 12 occurs as part of his concern for God's righteousness being shown in Christian living among those who are members of the body of Christ. He urges that the gifts to various members of

the body differ, therefore we must use them so that a particular gift function is present in the life of the body. He provides an illustrative list of gifts.

2. *1 Corinthians 12, 13.* Paul in this letter is addressing some of the concerns and issues raised by the Corinthian church, with its membership highly influenced by the pagan background of the city environment. His discussion of spiritual gifts needs to be understood in this context. Corinth was a city where trances, visions, speaking in unknown languages, and other ecstatic experiences were highly regarded among the pagans as being of particular significance and value. Paul wants to make certain the Christians are informed. He wants them to understand that all gifts of the Holy Spirit are for the common good of the body, which has many members with different functions. Any discussion as to which gifts are most important is irrelevant, for the body needs all its gifts and their functions. If one is going to talk about something being more important, it is the excellent way of love which is a gift to all members of the body. No one is without the capacity and gift to love. Without love, the other gifts are hollow and worthless.

3. *Ephesians 4:1-16.* The letter to the Ephesians is an interesting one. You may want to do some background reading about it in a Bible dictionary or a commentary. In substance it is an explanation of God's purpose in reuniting all things through Christ. One cannot understand God's purpose without considering the nature of the church as the body of Christ, an extension of the incarnation. Christ continues to accomplish his ministry of reconciliation through the church. Christians must bring unity to the body of Christ through love, understanding, and mutual service; then they can move with impact into a sinful, broken, disordered world. The passage concerning spiritual gifts contains a list of gifts which are essential for getting the members of the body ready for service and ministry. Through use of the gifts, the body will be built up to maturity, joined and knit together in unity of the faith.

4. *1 Peter 4:7-11.* This short epistle is written to Christians under severe persecution. They need encouragement during a period of great stress, tension, and threat. The key idea of the epistle is hope. Christians have a living hope in Christ who has redeemed them. He will sustain them and reward them. Their salvation is sure. In the

meantime they must develop lifestyles which are worthy of this hope. They must submit themselves to the will of God for their lives. These few verses about gifts are written for these persecuted people. Their love for one another must be genuine and abiding. Their spiritual gifts should be used for one another. Everything that is done should glorify God.

Take a few moments to reflect on some of the insights you have gained from your reading. What have you learned about spiritual gifts?

Some Issues Highlighted

There is probably much we do not understand about spiritual gifts, but we need to keep seeking insight and understanding. We as the body of Christ are missing a great source of strength if we do not develop and use the gifts which the Spirit has given us. Perhaps highlighting some issues will cause you to do some further thinking and exploration.

The Range of Spiritual Gifts

Because the lists of spiritual gifts contained in the passages we read are different, there is reason to believe that these lists are illustrative rather than exhaustive. Gifts needed in the twentieth- and twenty-first century church to build up the body and to accomplish ministry may be very different from those needed in Jerusalem, Antioch, Ephesus, Corinth, and Rome in the first century.

To think that we have a complete list, even if we combine all of those mentioned in Scripture, would be presumptuous on our part, given what we know about the character of the Holy Spirit. Jesus likened the working of the Spirit to the wind which we hear, but it blows where it will and we are uncertain where it comes from or where it is going. So it is with those who are born of the Spirit.

It is likely more appropriate to think of the range of spiritual gifts in terms of what is needed by the church, in order to be growing toward maturity and to be reaching out in ministry and service. Surely the Spirit will give the gifts that are necessary to be and do what God has intended.

Our challenge then is to avoid cutting off too narrowly the list of gifts. We hear this viewpoint voiced sometimes by Christians who believe they have none of the gifts listed in the Bible, therefore they are released from responsibility. That is not the case. All Christians have the gifts necessary to live in mutual love and to give glory to God. We must discover the gifts that God has entrusted to each one so that they can be maximized in building up the body, whether that be primarily in a leader or a follower position—or for most of us, both.

Spiritual Gifts and Talents

While there seems to be an obvious relationship between spiritual gifts and personal talents, we may at times need to distinguish between the two. There are talented people who never give any thought to using their abilities in ministry and service. I believe a talent becomes a spiritual gift when it is given in faith to Christ, surrendered to the control of the Holy Spirit, and used within the fellowship of the Christian community for service.

I have had students in my seminary classes who talk about rather dramatic changes in their talents and abilities which occurred at the time they committed their lives to Jesus. At that point they became aware of strength, depth, and power related to their talents which they had not known or experienced before. It was almost as if it were a new ability altogether. Perhaps you have had such an experience or know someone who would tell this kind of story.

I have also had persons share with me that they believe they have been given a spiritual gift for a specific challenge. It was not something they had previously done. In one case the person said, "I had no inclination for it. The gift came. When the challenge was over, the gift was soon gone."

This short-lived kind of spiritual gift seems to differ from natural talents, which are much more enduring. Of course, persons may have talents which are undiscovered or at least undeveloped until a later life experience, but once developed, they seem to endure. This enduring factor seems not always to be present with spiritual gifts, which on occasion seem to come and go more quickly.

It is true that our natural talents and abilities, when submitted to the Holy Spirit, become empowered gifts within the life of the Christian community. A talent can become a spiritual gift. It also seems wise to be open to the possibility that a spiritual gift can occur quite apart from talent if the need within the church is there.

Abuses of Spiritual Gifts

The active presence of the Holy Spirit in our midst can be blocked or misused. Perhaps the first blockage occurs when the church tries to exist and accomplish its mission as if there were no Spirit. Ignoring or even denying the existence of the Spirit prevents the full empowering action of the Spirit among us. God created us free to say yes or no. We are free to be open to the Spirit, but we are also free to say no!

A second abuse of spiritual giftedness is to use the gifts for the wrong reasons. To me this is a complicated dynamic. I believe spiritual gifts are given at a time when we are committed members of the body fully intending to employ the gifts with integrity for the building up of the body. But as human beings, we are often most vulnerable to sin at the points of our greatest strengths. Sometimes in very subtle ways we become led astray. We lose sight of why the gift was given. Our own individual purposes supplant the well-being of the body and its mission. Although not necessarily so, this change can occur without our conscious awareness. We may believe that we are continuing to serve the body at the very time we are contributing to its brokenness and pain.

When the mass suicide of the People's Temple movement occurred in Guyana, many persons responded with exclamations. "Incredible!" "Unbelievable!" "Unfathomable!" But it happened. It could be that Jim Jones began as a committed leader, using gifts genuinely bestowed by the Spirit, but over time went radically wrong.

All members of the body are charged to use their own gifts responsibly. Beyond our own judgment, we need one another to keep perspective on the ways we are using our gifts. Proper use of gifts to glorify God belongs to the whole body. Leaders seem to be in particularly vulnerable positions. Others are willing to follow their leading, yet they are frequently not willing to engage in dialogue and give negative or corrective feedback. Leaders may have to labor unusually hard to obtain the feedback they need.

A third abuse of spiritual gifts is elevating the value of one or two gifts above others. Because gifts are rooted in being the body of Christ and we are all members one of another, there is no way that one gift is more valuable than others. Just as no member of the body is more precious in God's sight than another, no gift is more worthy. All gifts are given for the body's well-being in its readiness and performance of ministry. The mini-gifts as well as the maxi-gifts are needed. Without each one, the full functioning of the body is diluted.

Perhaps in our computerized environment we have a new appreciation for the small and minuscule being of strategic importance. Entire space flights have been cancelled because of the malfunction of a tiny microchip. Until all the parts are operating properly, it would be unsafe to launch the flight.

The gifts which many leaders possess are often impressive. Their particular gift-mix combinations may stand out, overshadowing others. This is true, but as we have pointed out, leaders do not exist or function in a vacuum. Their gifts can only be used to full potential as other persons use theirs in response and relationship. Leadership happens in the betweenness. There is no greater worth or value. All are significantly important in being the body of Christ and in carrying out God's mission.

These are three abuses which can happen in relationship to gifts given by the Spirit. You may be able to think of others which have even greater significance in your life or within the context of your church congregation.

Cultivating Spiritual Gifts

Although the Spirit is the source and giver of spiritual gifts, these gifts are only on occasion given in developed form. More often they seem to be embedded as seeds in the lives of members of the body. These gifts have to be nurtured and cultivated over time. The whole body is responsible for this process.

Sometimes the process begins by helping body members discover their gifts. They may not be aware of the gifts they have or they may not realize that their gift can be used to build up the entire body. Some churches have found a workbook entitled *Discover Your Gifts*[1] to be helpful. Groups can use this manual to guide them in defining and understanding spiritual gifts, exploring biblical foundations in some depth, discovering and identifying gifts, confirming gifts, exploring unused gifts, and locating a place of service in the body of Christ. The manual also contains key questions with answers, studies of specific gifts, and a resource list. Whether this particular manual is used or not, the nurturing process is crucial.

Small churches seem to have some advantages. People know each other well. If they are made aware of the importance of helping each other in the process of discovering spiritual gifts, they can draw on the knowledge they have of one another and the needs of the church to help them acknowledge and draw forth spiritual gifts which perhaps are unrecognized or unexplored.

Small churches often struggle to find enough members to do everything that needs to be accomplished in order to maintain the life of the church and to extend beyond themselves in mission. Persons whose gifts are not fully developed may find an eager welcome to plunge in and get started.

I am often reminded of my own experiences growing up in rural Colorado, where I sang solos, played the organ, helped with Sunday church school, and taught vacation Bible school—more because I was needed than because my gifts were developed to the point where they had any polish. I am grateful for those opportunities. They have contributed in large measure to who I am today within the body of Christ.

The cultivating process may have to be more intentional in large churches, but it is just as necessary. Barriers will have to be overcome. Perhaps two illustrations will serve to show ways which two large churches employed to help persons discover and cultivate gifts.

One church had well-trained teachers in its active Sunday church school program. In addition, the church recruited assistants who moved through stages of helping with routine things until the recruits felt able to do some teaching, such as telling a story. Finally, the assistants moved into serving as substitutes and eventually into classes of their own on a regular, rotating basis.

The other church was in a university town. This church selected two students each year to serve on the diaconate board, with full participation in the spiritual care of the congregation. Experienced persons on the board mentored them. These are two ways larger churches have helped persons discover and cultivate gifts. There is no question in both cases that the persons involved learned something about their gifts and the leadership process.

Spiritual Gifts and Stewardship

The passage in 1 Peter presents a challenge that persons should use whatever spiritual gifts they have been given. It seems simple enough if each person has only one gift for which to be responsible. In my experience such is generally not the case, particularly if gifts are interpreted broadly. I have met primarily multi-gifted persons. They may not see or believe that they are multi-gifted, but in working alongside them I have discovered that they are.

One woman I knew thought her only gift was in organizing and implementing church dinners. She did it very well. As I came to know her, I learned that she also had abundant gifts in financial stewardship, significant caring expressions toward others, evangelistic witness, and hospitality in her home.

The question that most Christians face is how to be faithful stewards of the gifts they have been given. The most appropriate answers to questions of gift stewardship are not always obvious. It would be clearcut if we could say, "Use all of your gifts to their maximum capacity." Some multigifted people have adopted that principle and have had less than optimal results. Some have spread themselves so thin that they rarely use their gifts in quality ways. Others have spent so much energy in using their gifts that they have suffered from burnout. A few have invested so much of themselves that they have become resentful at having "overgiven." The answer cannot be a blanket "use your gifts to the maximum" for everyone.

We probably can never arrive at a precise principle that fits all persons. How gifts are used seems to be a matter for both individual and community decision making. There are many factors to consider. We must think about the well-being of the body and of the individuals who are that body. If one person has exercised a gift for many years, it may be time to allow new persons an opportunity to practice and develop what for them is a newly developed gift. Always our major criteria must be: Are the members of the church being equipped for ministry in an effective way? Is the body being strengthened and built up? Are we using our gifts to support and to be a means of God's grace to one another? Are we giving glory to God in the way we are using our gifts? If our response to these questions is, "Yes, we are doing the best we can do," then we can be assured that within our capacities to judge, we are being faithful stewards of our spiritual gifts.

We need to take seriously the link between leadership and spiritual gifts in the life of local congregations. Some present practices might need to change. We will probably need to invest more energies in understanding the meaning and purpose of spiritual gifts. We would consider the issues and walk alongside one another as we each try to identify the gifts in our own lives. We would try to formulate a picture of the various gifts the Spirit has entrusted to this congregation. As that picture emerges, we will gain a clearer and more complete sense of the form God's mission is to take in this particular body of believers. We will know where the leadership process is taking us and be able to contribute our gifts as leaders or as followers when the time is right.

CHAPTER 4

Lifelong Pilgrims in Church Leadership

The natural talents and skills we use in leadership begin early in life. Many of these become spiritual gifts to be used in the life and mission of the church as we grow in maturity in our Christian walk.

The Growth of Leaders

A pastor in announcing the birth of a baby into a church family graphically announced, "The Williams family has welcomed a new dictator into its midst this week." He paused a moment as the congregation stared at him quizzically, then continued, "The greatest dictators in the world are babies." He moved on to another announcement, but my mind was captured by his comments. My first response was to block out everything he had said except the fact that there was a new Williams baby. "Infants, after all, are so helpless and dependent. There is no way they can be dictators." My thoughts continued to race through my own experience. Our first child brought immediate change into our family. Someone had to make sure she was fed at the proper times. She needed a schedule for sleeping. One of her needs after another impinged on my previous way of

42 DEVELOPING LEADERSHIP IN THE TEACHING CHURCH

living. I had to adjust my life in relationship to hers. Later our son was born and more change entered our family life. His tiny being, with all of his physical and emotional needs, had an impact on my life. I decided that I would likely not make an announcement referring to a baby as a dictator but I recognized a level of truth in what the pastor was saying. If we take the needs of babies seriously, they do change our patterns of living. Sometimes in our efforts to recognize their dependency, we may ignore the extent of the influence infants exert. A leader is sometimes defined as "one who exerts influence." If so, then the roots of leadership lie in these early life experiences.

Infants and Toddlers

Babies are just beginning to learn about leading and following. They have a lifetime of lessons to learn. They usually begin their lessons through engaging in various kinds of interactions with their parents.

Parents soon learn to distinguish among their baby's cries. One cry marked with intensity calls forth immediate attention; another elicits only a casual response as the parent picks up a dropped toy; a third is ignored as the parent waits for sleep to win over the wailing protest. As such experiences accumulate over days, months, and a year, the baby becomes a toddler who continues the pilgrimage of learning about the give-and-take involved in influencing and being influenced by others. The learning process is rarely smooth. Inevitable pitfalls and snags seem to lurk around the corners of even the most innocuous interchanges.

I was sitting in a shopping mall waiting for some members of my family and focused my attention on a young family who had purchased some soft drinks and stopped while they were enjoying them. A nearly two-year-old girl sat in a stroller; her four-year-old brother perched on the fountain edge next to the stroller. Mom and Dad sat on a bench close by. The brother watched his young sister struggle clumsily with the cup and the straw. He moved in to help her. He took her cup, put the straw in his mouth and drew a mouthful. "Like that," he said. The sister smiled, clapped her hands, and tried it. "Not like that," big brother kibitzed. "Like this," he explained, taking another big drink. The third time this scenario repeated itself, little sister began her protest. Soon Mom moved in and everything was settled—almost settled! Little sister looked at big brother smugly as she took total control of her cup. Big brother gave her a quick return glare and moved to the other side of the bench out of her sight.

We learn much about leadership and followership in our families. We begin building a lifelog of experiences which inform us about such things as power, control, cooperation, manipulation, persuasion, submission, rebellion, defiance, and assent. Long before we have heard these words, we have experiences which supply us with their meanings. We gain a whole set of feelings which emerge when we find ourselves in situations where we have to make decisions about leading and following.

For most of us there was a safety as we learned about leadership in the family context. We made mistakes. On occasion our choices and behavior even resulted in punishment. Yet we still belonged to the family. We were part of it.

Elementary School Years

The school years which introduce outside peer relationships are another matter. Using the above illustration, a brother may exploit and treat his sister unfairly but they remain brother and sister. Tomorrow or the next day she may be the one to infringe upon his rights; yet they continue as family members together. It is more complicated in the school setting. If leadership moves with others aren't well negotiated, one can end up without a friend—for a day or two, or longer.

I was working in our garden as two elementary neighborhood friends, Pam and Joy, were playing. Pam seemed to be making the majority of the suggestions regulating their play. Joy followed along for a period of time. Eventually she made her own observations as to how things ought to be done. Her suggestion reversed or negated some things Pam had already set in motion. Pam stood her ground and declared, "We're already doing it MY WAY." Joy tried to build a case, but Pam continued to shake her head, "No." Suddenly Joy turned away, saying "I'm going home."

Pam: "You're not supposed to cross the street without me."
Joy: "I don't care. I can do it myself. I'm going home."
Pam: "You're mean."

Joy: "I am not. YOU'RE mean. You just always have to have your own way. I don't even like you anymore."
Pam: "I don't like you, either. See if I care if you go home."
Joy: "Who gives a care?"

She walked to the crosswalk, gave a quick check for cars, crossed the street, and ran down the block for home. Pam stayed in the schoolyard a few minutes, pushing stones around with a stick. Later she threw the stick on the ground, crossed the street, and walked to her own home. For several days they played with other friends. Eventually they found their way together again in the schoolyard.

We all have our own histories of childhood learning about leadership. We have friendships like Pam and Joy; we move into the more structured setting of school; we add clubs and sports; we attend church activities. Through it all we gain courage, we become cautious, we grow in judgment.

Youth

Our feelings and understandings about leadership experiences continue to build. The teen years broaden and deepen our learning. We are even more on our own. The family setting doesn't provide as much security, for youth are attempting to act independently of the home. Relating more intensely to persons of the opposite sex adds to the complexity of leadership dynamics. Cultural roles and expectations exert a certain amount of pressure. Males are supposed to behave in certain ways and assume given responsibilities. Females are expected to define themselves differently.

We live today in a period when many cultural, sex-role stereotypes are being challenged, but most of us can still relate to these kinds of pressures in our own lives. Leadership for males can operate in expected arenas and ways, while females often guide their leadership behavior by another set of expectations. Although clearly defined sexuality roles are being challenged, there is much which remains. For example, females who are "too aggressive and assertive" can meet with much greater resistance than do males standing for the same cause and exhibiting similar behavior. Traditionally, men have been expected to assume more straightforward and assertive leadership roles except in areas related to emotions and in nurturing relationships, where women are freer to excel.

Adolescence is a period for mastering these kinds of subtleties related to leadership issues, because the adult world lies just across the threshold. Although the male/female dynamic has been highlighted, there are many other leadership dynamics youth are attempting to master. They often find themselves struggling with the meaning of influence and power. How much will I try to influence others? To what extent will I allow others to influence me? Teenagers are constantly moving from one situation to another where they have to face these questions.

Young Adults

Young adults have to exert leadership skills they have developed in many areas of life—family, further training or education, jobs, close relationships or marriage, civic and church responsibilities. Although having reached the adult world at many levels, young adults may be treated in condescending, paternalistic ways by midlifers and senior citizens who are resisting the entrance of new persons into what has become a comfortable structure.

Occasionally the opposite happens. More leadership responsibility is handed to young adults than they are ready to assume. In one church a group of persons met to express their concern about issues of peace and the buildup of nuclear weapons. They decided to form a task force to operate within the life of the church and to reach out into the community. A young, single-parent father had joined the group. They selected him to lead the task force. "I'm concerned about these issues. I want my son to have a chance to live in a world of peace," he explained, "but I've never chaired a committee before. I don't even know where to begin. Is there someone who will help me?" He soon had a volunteer midlifer to walk alongside him.

Midlife Adults

Midlife persons have leadership agendas to learn. They have to give up styles of parental leadership which were necessary when their children were small. At the same time they find themselves in demand to fill other leadership positions being vacated by older persons who no longer have energy or interest to continue. The tendency to become overloaded with too many leadership responsibilities is a temptation for many midlife persons. It can be difficult to maintain focus. The outward direction of energy can lead to serious depletion, with no good or even adequate ways for renewal.

Some persons may arrive in midlife believing they have little or nothing to contribute as leaders. They tend to see everyone else as having more gifts, better skills, superior knowledge. They move toward the fringes of life involvements and may eventually become dropouts altogether. Midlifers have much to learn and the lessons may be painful at times.

Older Adults

One would be tempted to believe that when it comes to leadership, older adults surely have an edge. They must already have mastered everything there is to know. Obviously this is a period for coasting. Such is not the case. Every life stage presents its challenges. The senior years are no exception. Older adults have to learn the delicate balance of giving up much leadership responsibility to younger persons, yet retaining enough to maintain their own well-being. They have to discover ways to leave the leadership scene so that younger persons do not feel dominated and oppressed by their presence, yet to remain available so that when they are needed, they are there if possible. The challenges which come with senior years are difficult. They are anything but routine and simple. They come at a time when discernment as to the best way "to be and do" is complicated by many factors. When one would wish for easy and clearcut answers, they are not there. Instead, older adults have to hammer away at the best possible ways to address complex issues.

The Church Undergirds the Leadership Pilgrimage

What are the implications for the church's ministry if we recognize that leadership issues are faced by each person at every stage of life development?

It seems apparent that we must challenge any present views of leadership training that focus on adults as if they are the exclusive target for this strategic area of leadership development. We must expand our thinking to include the fact that even young children are learning to be leaders. The process of leadership learning is a lifelong pilgrimage. Each life age has its unique challenges to be addressed.

We likely do the most to cultivate the leadership potential of the very young by offering parent education, which enlightens parents with regard to ways of respecting the uniqueness of their children's personhoods. We can help parents learn to understand and to appreciate the developmental processes through which children move on their way toward autonomy and independent adulthood. While the stages may bring annoyance and frustration into the lives of parents, it may help them to be more tolerant if they understand what the children are working on in terms of their own development.

For example, two-year-olds are recognized for their stubborn persistence in saying, "No" at every turn. They add to their no's demands like, "Me do it myself" and claims to ownership when they scream, "Mine!"

Parents can be made aware that while this stage can bring its frustration, children are busy learning that they are independent small persons in a great big world. They are claiming their human potential to think, to choose, to possess, to exercise control over others, to reject control, and to value special things. All of these processes when developed are necessary for adult living, and they are requisites for participation in the leading/following dynamic which inevitably accompanies human relationships. The problem is that two-year-olds have very little experience. From an adult viewpoint they often say no to the wrong things. They frequently seem inconsistent. Sometimes they are yelling, "No!" at the very time they are doing the exact thing they are protesting. If parents understand the process, they can sensitively set limits and boundaries and, when there is no reason, simply withdraw from interference with the child's own exploration.

With many day care programs being run by churches or at least using church facilities, we have an opportunity to advocate that young children be provided with settings to explore their world of self, relationships, and things in ways that build a healthy initial set of leadership skills which they can continue to draw on throughout a lifetime.

As children move into their school years, our ministry among them is likely to be more direct if they participate in our programming either for age groups or for families. Throughout the school years, children need to continue their learning about relationships and communication. They can begin to develop appreciation and skills which help them communicate their messages clearly. Initial evaluations as to the impact of their communication with other persons can be done. Leadership issues such as when to forge out on one's own and when to follow are familiar territory to children as they try to carve their ways in neighborhood and school groups.

Bible teaching for children consistently needs to be linked to their life experiences. There is value in teaching about the lives of great leaders in the Bible. Beyond that, there is much we can do to help children see that humans, including those whose stories are in the Bible, have through history felt much the same as we feel today. Their ways of relating and communicating to one another brought consequences similar to those we experience today. Our contexts and circumstances approaching the twenty-first century seem like a totally different world, but human interactions are much the same.

Youth are continuing to build on their early life learnings. They can, however, reflect and analyze at deeper levels. Their increasing powers to think abstractly open new vistas of understanding. They are also increasing in their empathetic capabilities to see life as others see it.

Following encounters with other persons, youth may need an opportunity to reflect on what happened. They may lean on adults who have the gifts of understanding and patient listening. The adults must be sensitive. Sometimes they will be needed in an overt, active, involved way; at other times, distance may be called for.

During the adult years, learning to be involved more effectively in the leadership processes continues to be an issue. When to be leader, when to be follower, what kind of leader to be in specific situations, sharpening communication skills, unlearning ineffective patterns acquired at earlier stages, how to keep from being overloaded, how to relinquish leadership gracefully, undergirding leadership with a solid Christian ethical base—all these are adult challenges to be addressed. The church needs to provide a training ministry to help with the process.

The ministry of the church needs to include all ages when it is directed toward nurturing its leadership. New models and approaches may prove to accomplish our goals more adequately than those we have relied on in the past.

Small churches where people are known and where opportunities abound have some distinct advantages built into their context. Maximizing on learning from this situation, rather than taking it for granted, is essential if the potential of the small church is to blossom.

All churches need quality leadership; all persons have lifetime leadership challenges to learn. Bringing the two together in creative, productive ways is a challenge for the church's ministry.

5
CHAPTER

Creating a Climate for Church Leadership Commitment

Where does the church secure its leadership? Are there always persons who are willing and available to serve? Let's consider two churches.

Nearly everyone in town has heard about good things happening in "Church Alive." There are two services of worship on Sunday morning and there are plans to start a third one in the fall. A special task force is working on plans for increasing available space. A new building is one option; another, the use of an elementary school building closed two years ago by the local school board. People are congregating at the church building every day for some reason. There are activities for all age groups and for people with varied interests and concerns; they are well attended. The life of this church extends beyond its own walls as the members move out in service as individuals or in mission groups. An atmosphere of vitality permeates Church Alive. The members seem to enjoy being together. They arrive on time with warm greetings and hugs. They stay after meetings to engage in spirited conversation. It is a common pattern for them to make contact with one another quite apart from regularly scheduled meetings. People feel that important things are going on at Church Alive. They like being a part of it. They believe that the future for Church Alive holds significant challenges, but they are confident they have the resources to meet them. They are committed to Church Alive's ministry in very concrete ways. They are willing to invest time, energy, and financial resources to contribute to the growth and well-being of Church Alive.

Just over a mile away from the vital, active scene of Church Alive is the impressive building of "Church Adrift." By external appearances it would be logical to assume that congregational life is strong and healthy here, too. The stone building with its picturesque stained-glass windows is obviously well cared for; the tastefully landscaped grounds have without question received attention. The sealer on the parking lot appears to have been recently applied. But the internal life of this congregation is a different matter. At worship services the front pews are conspicuously vacant. Over time one notices that attendance is irregular except for a small nucleus. There is a marked tone of discouragement. Involvement seems to stem from feelings of obligation and duty. Activities beyond the regular service of worship are sparsely attended. Some well-planned programs which seem to have potential and value never actually materialize because church members are unwilling to commit themselves to being present. The pastor and those involved in positions to make decisions feel unsupported. They frequently complain that no one is committed. It's as if nobody really cares much what happens at the church. Members contribute enough to take good care of the church building and the grounds. They see that the pastor and other members of the staff are well paid. But there is definitely not much excitement around Church Adrift. One has the distinct impression that unless new life comes from somewhere, further decline will lead to more severe problems. The members often recall that things used to be better at Church Adrift. They would like to recapture the days when everyone was involved. The Sunday church school was the largest in town; the youth groups were known to the whole community; the choir program was outstanding; the large sanctuary was full to overflowing. No one seems to know how to get back to that kind of health. Who would put in the time and energy?

You may be able to name the parallel churches to Church Alive and Church Adrift in your community. You may be capable of tracing the history of your own church. Perhaps like Church Adrift, your congregation, too, has experienced a slow but steady decline. More encouragingly, your church may have experienced a renewal that has brought transformation from a situation similar to Church Adrift to one more like Church Alive. Some of us may be able to see parts of our church life that are vital and alive, while other parts are struggling and adrift. Some of us may be fearful that the decline among the membership of our church is so ingrained that eventually it will become "Church Severely Sick" or even "Church Dead."

When we consider leadership issues we discover that they are closely intertwined with the overall health and vitality of the life of the congregation. A Church Alive-type congregation will usually find a ready supply of leaders. There is someone willing to tackle the most challenging and difficult of responsibilities and someone else who is willing to assume the seemingly insignificant behind-the-scenes tasks. If there is a leadership vacancy for which there seems to be some difficulty finding a volunteer, when the need is made known and gifts are considered, there is usually someone who says, "I'll be glad to do it." There may be a backlog of potential leaders to the extent that when some finish a term of responsibility, they really are free to back away for a period of time and move in new directions of service because there are other leaders present to take their place.

The enthusiasm which permeates congregational life seems to generate motivation to involvement and service. There is a contagion which seems to flow among the membership.

In contrast, Church Adrift-type congregations often struggle with maintaining a leadership supply. Every fall a crisis occurs when it is time to make sure there are sufficient church school teachers and youth leaders. The upcoming annual meeting creates panic among the nominating committee members, who have no idea where the people will come from to fill the slate of officers. The leaders who have faithfully been involved and given their time often find themselves discouraged and spent. In a sense they have over-given by trying to do the work of two, three, or four people. They have grown weary from the overload and need a respite. Reports that there are desperate needs to fill vacancies are often met with indifference or resistance. Some who agree to serve seem to communicate, "I'm feeling guilty, so I'll do it to get my term over and ease my conscience."

There isn't much long-term enthusiasm in Church Adrift. Discouragement seems to be the predominant contagious outlook which creeps from member to member, settling in deeper year by year.

A Positive Climate for Leadership

Through a major research study[1] we have learned some of the factors which are present in strong, vital, alive congregations. The four factors which have been identified, along with three others to be noted, are valuable pieces of information. They enlighten our understanding of what healthy church life is like. They increase our insight into the particular areas of church life which we can work to strengthen.

Cohesiveness

Healthy, vital churches demonstrate a high degree of cohesion. Cohesiveness in a group or organization is difficult to define. It is like the breeze which one feels and whose effects one can see, but which in itself escapes our vision. Cohesion has been called the social glue that holds a group together. When cohesion is high, the bonding is strong among the members. They like one another; they like being part of the group; they feel a loyalty and a commitment to contribute to the group's well-being; they are willing to live by the standards of the group. Membership means a great deal to persons involved in a highly cohesive church. They are willing to put their involvement in the church at top priority.

At some levels high cohesion seems just to happen on its own; but there are things we can do to nurture and cultivate high cohesion. Nancy and Ernest Bormann in their book *Effective Committees and Groups in the Church*[2] give some suggestions. They discuss seven steps that can be taken which include working at a clear, solid, identity; building and celebrating the tradition of the church; stressing and undergirding teamwork; recognizing quality work; setting clear and reachable goals; rewarding the entire community when a goal has been achieved. Other things could be done, but these ideas are a good beginning.

Mutual Support

Healthy vital churches report an awareness of mutual support. They know they are part of a team, each concerned about the well-being of the other. Support permeates the fabric of their relationship network as an ongoing process. It emerges not only in crunch spots or crises; support is also there in the normal times and the victories. Members feel accepted and liked; they feel heard and understood; they feel free to be themselves within the boundaries of membership definition. They understand that they are accountable to one another; yet they have confidence that when they are having trouble doing all that they are supposed to do, there are others who will walk alongside or even move in and carry the entire load.

Mutual support must be tended and nourished if it is to flourish. It often develops naturally along friendship lines, but in the church it must be extended beyond the persons to whom one feels close. Learning names and backgrounds helps to communicate to others that you care and are interested in them. Taking time to listen carefully and making certain common meanings have emerged demonstrates concern. The list of concrete behaviors which build support can be lengthy. More important is identifying the ways of showing support that seem most appropriate for your specific congregation. Making specific commitments to relate in supportive ways is important. It also helps to report to one another in some context so you can get a picture of how support is happening and so you can evaluate your progress and growth.

One of the interesting dynamics of support relationships is that supportive acts from one person to another are frequently returned by that person. Something like a smile often draws forth a reciprocal smile; similarly an act of support is reciprocated. It may take a long time; sometimes it is never returned. Often, however, a search shows that one supportive act has led to another—returned to the original giver or passed on to another in need. Mutual support is a valid and necessary ministry of the church.

Efficiency

Healthy, vital churches work with efficiency. They put their decision making, their planning, and their programming involvements together in ways that maximize the use of persons' energies and minimize their use of time. They are unwilling to come together and accomplish little or to drift along with no forethought given to direction or process.

It is important to note that efficiency does not rule out coming together for fun, socializing, and casual conversations. There is space for all of these, but when the time arrives to work together, efficient approaches are used. Efficiency is not to be equated with formal structures or processes. It is possible to be very informal, yet to operate in an efficient style.

Groups can be efficient in many ways. Being efficient usually involves some persons doing preliminary work and preparation prior to the time people come together. Their use of time in a meeting is monitored by leaders as well as by the entire group. They stick with the task at hand. Follow-up is carefully planned to assure that implementation happens, and to reduce unnecessary duplication of effort by group members.

Adaptability

Finally, healthy, vital churches sense the need and move ahead to adapt to change. Given the phenomenal rate of change in our world, this factor presents a rather formidable challenge. The content of our faith remains the same, but the manner in which it is applied to our ways of being the church and to our personal lives has to change. If we refuse to change or become paralyzed by the need to change, in a sense we contribute to distorting the meaning of our faith in our own day.

The four factors of high cohesion, mutual support, efficiency, and adaptability all characterize vital, healthy churches. Three other dynamics should be noted.

The Spirit's Presence

Vital, healthy, growing churches inevitably seem to have a renewed sense that the Spirit of God is moving in their midst, leading them to take risks to be what and where God wants them to be.

It seems that we sometimes lose sight of the fact that we are post-Pentecostal people. The Spirit is available to be Christ's presence among us. Disciplined prayer and Bible study help to prepare us for the leading of the Spirit, which may call us forth to greater risks than we normally would take on our own.

Small Groups

Churches which are experiencing renewed vitality nearly always have incorporated a significant small group ministry of some kind into their fellowship. A depth of sharing and a commitment to care for one another in concrete ways is built into the fabric of the group experience. There seem to be many patterns which can work to accomplish a small group ministry. The best way is the one which most adequately meets the needs of a specific congregation.

Leadership Core

A central core of concerned committed leaders can usually be identified in vital, healthy churches. They are persons who give of themselves in dedicated ways to seek direction, to initiate some movement, to enlist others, to ensure ongoing involvement. The stories of how these committed leader groups get started vary, but if a story is traced back far enough the account notes that one person shared with another the dream or hope that things could be different. These two shared with one another. In time, a core group formed.

To the degree that congregations are vital and healthy, leadership recruitment becomes easier. Working to increase the vitality of congregational life contributes to securing and maintaining a solid leadership structure.

Barriers to Leadership Recruitment

Unfortunately, even congregations with a great deal of vitality discover there are barriers to overcome in securing leaders. These barriers have to be acknowledged, understood, and addressed.

Time

Our environment is one in which many people find that time is their most precious life resource. There are not enough hours in the week to do what they have to do, are expected to do or want to do. They constantly feel pressured to make hard choices. Ideally they would like to be involved in many things. There are numerous activities that they would enjoy and believe in, but they have only a limited amount of time available.

Pluralism

Setting priorities in a pluralistic environment where there is such a smorgasbord of options is a monumental challenge. The choices are difficult because of the ambiguity which seems to permeate the process of choosing alternatives. Some options can usually be rejected; others can be placed in a mid-range of "nice, but not particularly appealing." Even when these alternatives have been eliminated, there may still be too many "appealing, exciting, and rewarding choices" to fit into one's life. So persons are faced with choices among "the goods." This situation always presents a life dilemma. What would I like to choose? What should I choose? Is there a best way?

Structure

For some persons, the structure of their lives is such that involvement in church leadership seems futile—particularly if they want to be regular in attendance and to contribute beyond the minimum expectation. Perhaps some examples may help to focus who some of these persons may be in your congregation. People who have jobs with changing shifts or which require them to travel a great deal fall into this category. Other kinds of job requirements can create similar circumstances. Some people have to place a high priority on health care. They may have an illness which demands a time-consuming regimen, or they may be confined with the care of a family member.

Depletion

More persons are involved in service jobs than ever before in history. Many of them find that they are constantly being asked to direct their life energy flow toward meeting the needs of others. In time spent outside their jobs they look for ways to renew and rebuild their own energy resources. For some of these people, opportunities to serve in church leadership positions may seem to them to be one more involvement which continues to drain and deplete them. They simply feel they "can't give any more," even though the opportunities sound worthwhile.

Low Self-Worth

Some persons hesitate to accept the invitation to involvement in leadership because they struggle with pervasive feelings of low self-worth. They simply don't believe that they have anything to contribute that someone else can't do substantially better. An observer may think there often appears to be no reality base to the self-worth struggles of a person who seems to be talented, attractive, and gracious in approach to others. But judgments about the self are deep internal evaluations growing from early life experiences. An "outsider" may not find such an assessment accurate, but it is likely to be firmly anchored in the belief system of the person who concludes, "I am not good enough to be a leader." Some even believe, "I am not good enough to be a follower. If people knew me, I'm not even good enough to belong to this church. I won't get involved."

Leadership recruitment for the church has to occur within the realities of modern life with all the barriers it presents. Time, a plurality of opportunities, restrictions from structure, depletion from continual service to others, and the questioning of self-worth—all present barriers to a positive response when persons are asked to accept the challenge to become involved in strategic leadership processes in the church.

Recruitment and Relationships

When we approach the task of recruiting persons to leadership positions, we must present the challenge in a way that their response is, "Yes, this is an involvement to which I want to commit myself."

Persons are more likely to be motivated positively if we keep four levels of relationships in mind. Each of these interacts with a person's motivation and decision to become involved in service. These four relationship levels are discussed in depth in a provocative book by Dr. Aaron Levenstein, *Why People Work*.[3]

Self

The first level is the person's self. We are more likely to say yes to involvement opportunities if we believe that there is a fit between our personhood and what we are being asked to do. We may ask the following questions: Does this opportunity utilize my gifts which I have been given and have developed? Does it give me a chance to practice and explore new aspects of my life abilities? Is there a reasonable possibility that I can do well what I am being asked to do? Will I likely be embarrassed or frustrated personally? Is this where God wants me, or do I feel God may be leading me in other directions? How guilty will I feel if I say no?

Interpersonal

The second level is the interpersonal. Most of us place a great deal of importance on our relationships with other persons. We ask such pertinent questions as: Will I be working with people I know and enjoy? Will I have the opportunity to meet and cultivate new friends? Are there people to whom I seem to have trouble relating? How will I handle having to work with them? Will this commitment build my relationships deeper and stronger or will it simply add another strain and stress?

Church

The third level is based on my commitment and loyalty to the church. We find something of our identity in the organizations to which we belong and in which we participate. For Christians, the church should be our faith family. When asked to assume some task, we need to ask: Does my involvement contribute to the well-being of the whole congregation? Will the church and its ministry be strengthened if I do this? Do the other members of my faith family agree that this place of service is best for me? Have we assessed our gifts so we have confidence that my involvement represents a quality decision?

Global

The fourth level is a global one. Many persons are concerned that their time and energy involvements in some small way bring a measure of healing and wholeness to humankind around the world. Contributing to the local congregation and people we know is important, but many like the assurance that what they do contributes to the building of God's kingdom around the world. Our questions are often vague and abstract. They may never come into clear focus: Will my efforts bring healing to my town, my state, my country, my world? Is what I am doing contributing to peace, love, and justice around the world rather than perpetuating provincial interests and imbalanced, unjust relationships? Am I acting as a member of the worldwide family of God?

These four levels may not be consciously considered by all persons. If we can raise them in our leadership education, they can touch deep chords in persons' lives and provide them with some solid standards against which to consider carefully the challenge: "Our church needs you. Are you willing to commit yourself?"

Motivation for involvement in leadership is complex and it can be difficult. It seems to occur best in a healthy organizational climate where peoples' relationships are taken seriously. There are inevitable barriers which have to be overcome.

6
CHAPTER

Church Leadership in Action

Some persons seem to stand out as leaders. A newly formed group comes together with the intention of charting its direction and selecting its leaders. Before the group has made any kind of formal decision, it is often possible to predict that certain persons will be chosen as leaders of the group—or if not formally named, powerful persons will function as leaders in the group.

If we reflect on our various experiences, it probably won't take us too long to realize some important truths in the statement: "The leadership balance in a group is achieved over time. It does not happen in an instant; nor does it remain the same. It is ever changing."

Stages of Leadership

Scholars have helped us see that leaders emerge through a series of stages.[1] These stages can often be identified in group life.

Stage One

An appropriate name for stage one seems to be withdrawal. That may surprise us. During this stage a number of people are identified as being persons who will not serve as leaders. Some of these people are reserved, quiet persons who seem to prefer operating in a follower role. Others, however, are persons who act and look as though they would make fine leaders; but they make it known somehow that they are not available. Time is often an issue. They are already overloaded. Interest can be an issue. It might be stated in this way: "I am concerned about this group and its future; but there are other priorities in my life, too. I'm willing to give some energy here, but not enough to take a major leadership role." During stage one the withdrawal of persons from being chosen as leader can take many forms. You will learn more about it if you watch it in action in the groups to which you belong. You may even see a person try to withdraw; the group pushes him or her to reconsider; the person reluctantly accepts. In the process of carrying out the responsibilities, such a person does only a halfhearted job. The other group members carp and criticize. Think about the idea that the problem began in stage one and lies much deeper than one person not carrying through on a responsibility.

Stage Two

Stage two could be called identification. During this stage the group identifies who the possible leaders are. Usually these are persons who are active participants, who care about the group, who believe in its goals, and who have some experience. Sometimes a leader is immediately apparent. This person is the obvious choice of the group and the person affirms the rightness of that choice from a self-perspective.

In contrast, the process can be very complex. Two, three, or even more persons may seem like equally possible choices. Often people who have withdrawn earlier lend quick support to someone else to assure that the challenge won't come back to them, this time with more emotional appeal.

Sometimes a single individual does not emerge. The group may find that selecting co-leaders is a good alternative. Co-leadership can add vitality to a group if the leaders work together well as a team and the group responds to and owns their leadership.

Stage Three

Finally, when it is possible to identify that certain persons are the leader(s), then stage three has come. This stage could be called stabilization. The leaders have been chosen. Now the group has to learn how to work together. Sometimes the process of working as a group happens so smoothly that people give it little thought. In other instances it is marked by many abortive attempts before the patterns that really will work to the satisfaction of group members have emerged. Sometimes the frustration level gets so high that leaders give up and literally resign from the position or functionally withdraw until other group members move in to see that the job gets done. It may be that a contingency of followers in the group drop out.

One myth that some persons cling to about leadership is that when the leader or leaders have been chosen, the major part of the work is done. "Our church has elected a full slate of new officers, so they can do the work for this year." Leaders who have been chosen in this fashion may be dreading the year ahead. They have no idea how they will pull things off. They are uncertain of support from the followers, who seem to be sitting comfortably in their places waiting for things to happen.

The fallacy in the myth can perhaps be understood most graphically if we think about our church life as something like a sports team. We would all say, "How foolish!" if the team elected its captains and then all but the chosen captains went to the sidelines. Rather, we expect to see that team move into action with all members continuing to give time and energy to play the game.

Perhaps thinking of ourselves as a team will give us some clues as to how to make the body of Christ with all of its diversity function as a unity. There are some body organs which are more crucial than others. We can have a tooth pulled, a leg amputated, or a kidney removed; but we have to have a brain, a heart, and a liver. Even organs in the latter group must be sustained by each other's functioning.

Leaders cannot "run the church" by themselves and have a healthy outcome. That's why understanding leadership is so crucial. Leadership belongs to all members. It is shared among everyone. When one speaks, others must listen. When a decision is made by the group, it belongs to all the members to see that it is implemented. This does not mean that all members have to participate in getting it done—but rather to outline and to agree on a way.

Leader Styles

There is no pattern which guarantees that leaders and followers can work out a harmonious, effective leadership balance. Two critical factors are that leaders have different styles and followers have different needs.[2] The needs of the group have to come together with the styles of the leaders in a productive mix. That mix may look very different from group to group and from church to church. The test is whether the mission of the church is being advanced and whether healthy, restored relationships are being built and maintained.

Most of us, when we are assigned or end up in the position of leader, have ways of behaving that seem comfortable to us. We call these ways of behaving "leader styles." There are a number of ways to categorize leader styles.

Some leaders use a *task style*. They want to get the job done. They know what the goal is and have a plan for reaching it. They often tell the members of the group how they fit into the plan and what they should do. These leaders push the group until the goal is reached.

Some leaders use a *relational, social style.* Their major concern has to do with the quality of relationships in the group—the leader's relationship with group members and their relationships among one another. No goal should be so important that it hurts or destroys the relationship fabric of the group. In fact, reaching the goal should be a way of strengthening relationships.

Some leaders use a *charismatic style,* which leans heavily on their own personality. Group members may even join the group because they are attracted to the leader. Leaders who use this style are usually talkative and persuasive; they are gregarious and warm; they are involved and enthusiastic. The goal will be reached because group members gather around the leader, and they move ahead together.

Some leaders use what has been called a *laissez faire style.* In a sense these persons are leaders in name only. They simply let the group run itself. The task may not get done if group members fail to move in and see that something happens. Relationships will get little attention beyond what group members themselves give to one another.

Some leaders use a *combination style.* They want very much to see the goal achieved. They hope that the group will succeed and move forward. At the same time they are unwilling to accomplish the goal at the expense of relationships. They, therefore, direct some energies toward building and sustaining a solid relational network. This style is demanding because the leader has to consider a number of different facets of group life.

Some leaders use a *prophetic style*. They are ahead of the status quo and place a challenge before the group members that their way of being and acting must be changed if their true identity is to be lived out. This style often engenders resistance because it carries a value judgment that the present is not good enough and that there is a way to find and to live with more integrity. Persons who lead as prophets may find only a small following who come with them, or at times they may stand alone having made their pronouncement.

Some leaders use a *catalyst style*. They have an ability to get things moving and arouse interest and enthusiasm. When a leader catalyst has stirred up the group life, things are definitely off dead center. The group is ready to begin toward its goal and care for its relationships.

Some leaders use a *servant style*. This style is rooted first in the desire of the person to serve others and only secondarily to lead. The test of a servant leader is whether the people being served are more whole, more free, more independent, more likely themselves to become servants to bring healing and wholeness to others. Another part of the test is that the effects on others beyond the group, particularly the disadvantaged, are that they, too, will benefit or at least not be further deprived.[3]

These are some ways to describe leader styles. There could be others. These can come together in individualized patterns which each person forges.

Most persons have a preferred leader style which usually works for them and with which they feel secure and comfortable. These styles have emerged through the give-and-take of life experiences. Persons have life-rooted reasons for having developed their styles.

When the preferred style fails to work, people may then move to another style which serves as a backup. Most of us have one, two, or possibly three backup styles. If none of our styles seem to be working for us and the group frustration mounts, we suffer our way through until our term is over or we may decide to quit.

There is much we can learn about leader styles. Leader styles can be analyzed and understood. We can even learn new behaviors which are more common to other styles than our own. We are not stuck with our style forever. As we expand our leader behaviors, we can be more flexible in meeting the needs of the group.

Group Needs

Groups have at least three levels of needs. They need to have some significant success in reaching their goals; they need to have healthy relationships with one another; and they need to have a structure so that these two things can happen.

In order to reach the goals, the group has to make a series of decisions and carry them out. Group members have to secure information. If someone in the group has the information, it needs to be shared with everyone. If members have to go elsewhere to find information, then a plan for getting the information has to be devised. As decisions are being made, group members need to know the opinions and judgments of the others. Sometimes the decision-making process bogs down and has to be reinitiated and energized. At other times the group may feel overwhelmed because there is too much information. Someone needs to pull it together and summarize the salient points.

Healthy relationships are cultivated in a number of ways. Being listened to and understood by the group is crucial. If members are shy, they may need some encouragement. Hearing the group tell me I've done a good job or have been a valuable part of the team goes a long way in helping me feel that my membership in this group counts for something. When conflict emerges, group members may need to help each other heal any resulting hurts. In our group life we need to feel confident that relationships count.

The group needs structures that assure that goals will be achieved and relationships will be valued. Some persons may give thought to alternative structures which could be used. Some may identify when change and new ways of organizing are necessary. Group members can become ineffective and discouraged because they are trying to accomplish their goals through inappropriate and inadequate structures.

Groups have many needs. They seek leaders who will recognize and address their needs in healthy ways.

Achieving a Leadership Balance

Leaders have styles and groups have needs. Each leader is unique; every group is different. A group may remain the same in name and membership but changing needs make it seem like a totally new group.

Quality leadership happens when the styles of the leaders and the cooperating behaviors of the group members come together to meet the group needs. Some examples may help us understand how this happens.

A board of Christian education has changed only two members this year. Last year the board experimented with planning some creative summer programming for elementary and middle school children. Setting goals, planning, and making decisions all seemed to happen like a well-orchestrated cantata. The group used its previous experiences with vacation church school, day camp, weeklong camping, and Sunday church school as a base to create and build something new. An outsider would hardly be able to recognize that this group had a leader at all. Group members seemed to take turns at helping the board make its decisions. They checked feelings out with one another. The plan was implemented. Responses were positive and appreciative. With only some minor adjustments to address rough edges and to enhance quality at a point or two, the plan was ready to be used again another summer.

Recently the same board was approached to be a part of an ecumenically sponsored effort to run a summer program the following year for the increasing number of Spanish-speaking children who have moved into the area with their immigrant families. The well-orchestrated process which emerged last year can hardly get off the ground. The leaders become crucial persons in this new situation. They have to decide what processes to use to get the board moving. There is much information that has to be secured. The leaders have to draw forth whatever information is in the group and go to outside sources for whatever else is needed. Given that board members have different views of ecumenically sponsored programs, there are perspectives to be shared and feelings to be considered. Not everyone would agree on the church's involvement in this endeavor. There have been previous ecumenical programs which have been dismal failures and a "waste" of church resources. Several are asking why this project would be different. There is much to be explored and progress seems to come slowly. It is hard to believe that this is the same group that worked together last year. The leaders who last year were able to share their power in very open ways with other group members find a new and difficult challenge this year.

Churches who have their goals clearly identified, who understand their mission, and who have worked at their relationships are ready for leaders whose styles push them toward making those goals happen. With good, forceful, visionary leaders and cooperative members, the mission may go forth in astonishing ways.

Other churches may have different needs. They have experienced a great deal of division, pain, and hurt. Their history has left them with deep and paralyzing wounds. These churches need leaders who are drawn to the relational aspects of community life. Energies directed toward understanding and healing will begin to rebuild a relational fabric. The primary goal has to become one of restoring wholeness in the body. Only small tasks related to outward mission may be accomplished for a time. To attempt more would perhaps be to add another failure.

Different needs call for different leader styles. It is helpful when churches clarify what they need, and leaders recognize to what extent their styles address those needs. Crucial questions for leaders are: Do my styles and my skills create a healthy mix with the needs of this group? When other styles and skills are needed, are the necessary resources in the group? Is this a situation where it seems to make sense, with God's help, to commit myself to a leader role? Are there other situations where my gifts and abilities might be more obediently and faithfully used in God's ministry?

Adequate answers to these kinds of questions arrived at by both the leaders and the members of the group will help to facilitate securing the best possible leadership mix and balance for a given group. It is a challenge which deserves thought, time, energy, and much, much prayer.

7
CHAPTER

Keys to Effective Church Leadership

For centuries people have been fascinated by outstanding leaders. How did they get to be where they are? Are they born with special talents and abilities? Did they happen to appear on life's historical stage when there was a need for them? These and other questions have been asked thousands of times over. Many and sundry attempts have been made to answer them.

Little attention has been given to followers. In many instances they have been described in a sentence or two as persons who were caught up by the magnetic power of the leader. With that kind of explanation, all attention is focused again on the leader.

We have seen in previous chapters that both leaders and followers are crucial if leadership is to happen. Like teachers who cannot teach if no one is present or open to learn, leaders cannot lead if no one will choose to follow.

Yet those who have sought to dissect the inner dynamics of leaders and how they come to be, have focused on an important truth aspect: Leaders are important people. They are in a very real way key people who set the tone for the entire group or organization. Their personal enthusiasm seems to be catching. They can undergird the process of building group health and vitality.

You may have been part of a group where the movement and tone has been in the opposite direction. Leaders can lose their enthusiasm. Their pessimism can seep through the membership. The entire group soon feels defeated.

If you have ever tried to reverse a negative group climate without being in some kind of leader position, you have probably found it very difficult if not impossible. Followers can exert great energy and devise intricate plans, but working around the negativism of leaders is formidable. On occasion, followers do succeed in turning the tone of a group around. Frequently this happens because leaders themselves respond to the urging of the members who are seeking to change the group climate.

Leaders are key persons. What makes them such crucial people in the life of the group? Is it who they are? Is it the situation? Is it what they do? Behavioral science research has helped us gain some clarity in answering these questions.

Leaders are often seen by group members as being special people with an unusual set of gifts. Group members may even say something like, "Oh, our leader was made for this job." There is, however, no established list of leader characteristics which can be applied from situation to situation. One leader may be talkative; another, more quiet-mannered. One may be described as "physically attractive"; another, as "quite plain." One may be forceful and dominant; another, gentle and supportive. If there were a Leader Hall of Fame complete with voices and facial expressions, the portraits would look and sound very different. A wide spectrum of personalities would be included.

Situations do make a difference. A leader who is outstandingly effective in one situation may flounder in another. Churches and ministers have experienced this phenomenon in pastoral leader changes. A combination that has worked well in one congregation does not guarantee that the pastor will perform effectively in another congregation.

There are ways that leaders behave which make a difference in their effectiveness. If we were to visit the imaginary Leader Hall of Fame and survey each one as to how he or she acted and what each did, we might very well discover a core of common behaviors.

It is not that all of these leaders would look alike in action. These behaviors can be incorporated into differing styles. The end products, however, are similar. Here are some of the key things in group life that effective leaders do.

Trust Building

Effective leaders work at establishing a climate of trust in the group.[1] They try to present themselves in such ways that the group members believe and place their confidence in them as leaders. Building trust among the membership is also important.

Leaders are more likely to be trusted if they are knowledgeable and competent. Leaders need to do their homework when it comes to having necessary information. Becoming informed happens through many avenues. Reading, interviewing, listening, observing are strategic processes. Of course, leaders bring to their position their own life experiences upon which they can draw.

Trust is built as leaders are dependable and reliable in their relationships with group members. When leaders actually do what they say they will do, trust grows. When leaders follow through on promises they have made, trust grows. When leaders time and again demonstrate that their words become lived out in action, trust grows. When leaders share with the group from their thoughts and feelings, trust grows.

Trust grows slowly in a bit-by-bit fashion. Gradually an environment which communicates "we trust each other in this group" develops. A trustworthy climate is a precious commodity in group life. It deserves extraordinary attention. Unfortunately, a trusting network can be torn apart much faster than it can be built. Effective leaders work at exploring and explaining mistakes, oversights, and insensitivities. Talking these inevitable negative happenings through brings understanding and clarity. Although there will be a strain in the trust area, the group realizes and relies on such understanding when hurtful things happen. There is a pattern and there are resources for handling them; they are not ignored.

When a climate of trust exists among people, there is a kind of group empowerment that takes place. Persons are freed from diverting their energies to wonderment, doubt, suspicion, and mistrust. They know that others can be counted and relied on to accept and support them even if they make a mistake. If they fail altogether, they are confident that they will have an opportunity to explore, to be understood, and to continue being embraced by the group.

Trust-building belongs to all the members of a group, but leaders do much to set the tone. Their relationship styles toward the group of warmth, acceptance, caring, involvement, and enthusiasm are core ingredients. Even members who struggle at deep internal levels with trust may eventually begin slowly to take the risk of trusting this group. In the process they may experience the kind of healing that extends into other life relationships beyond the group. They begin to believe that there are people who can be trusted.

Participation

Effective leaders attempt to communicate to all members of the group that they are important and that they count. Involvement and participation in the shaping of group life by all members becomes a priority.

The kind of participation being indicated here is not a superficial facade which provides opportunities for input and discussion where people have a chance to verbalize their opinions and feelings; but the actual direction of what happens in the group is determined by the leaders and perhaps two or three confidants. The input time provides an arena for venting and making known one's position, but the direction taken shows little or no change based on the members' views.

Rather the kind of participation associated with effective leaders is one where members are assured that they will not only be heard, but also that they can have a significant impact. How they see things, how they set priorities, and how they feel will all become part of the mix which is taken into consideration as the directions of the group are shaped. The influence is real. It has been shown that when members are free to participate in group and organizational life at significant levels, satisfaction is high; members are more responsible; commitment is strong; frustration with group life is low; and pride in their accomplishments is evident.[2]

Meaningful participation is more than a chance to talk. It is also preparing to take action as part of the group and then following through.

Leaders who want genuine participation by group members usually have to work at bringing it about. Most of us have so often been members of groups where we haven't felt much more than pawns, that we tend to respond reluctantly to the initial invitations to become active participants. Our thoughts may progress something like this: "Oh, sure, I've heard that before. They ask us for ideas, how we feel, what we think; but they don't really care. They have their minds made up anyway. What good does it do? They don't really want to listen to us." We may even add: "Besides, if I say anything important, I will end up doing all of the work. It pays to keep my mouth closed in this group." So there is prolonged silence broken only by a rather superficial input here and there, perhaps given to be polite or perhaps to test the leaders' integrity. Leaders may have to be involved in a rather long process of convincing group members that they will be taken seriously. In many ways leaders will have to communicate the message: "I want you to participate; I want you to work with me and the other members to shape this group; we are a team when it comes to group life. We will not lay a burdensome trip on one another. We will work together."

Being truly open to participation involves risk on the part of the leaders. It implies that power will to a great extent be shared by all the members of the group. Persons will differ as to how they believe the group should proceed. The leaders may be asked to move in directions they had not intended to go; they may be challenged to modify a time plan; they may be asked to accept the fact that a group has said, "No!" It takes a long time for leaders and group members to reach this kind of balance, but when it is achieved there are noticeable differences in the life of the group. Both commitment and creativity are more consistently present than in any group structures where a minority dominates and controls power.

Commitment is high because group members know that the quality of the group's life belongs to all of them. They are the ones who shape it. If the group is less than they think it should be, they have to take a look at themselves. In the church this kind of commitment can be freeing to the congregation, who in a whole new way has to face the facts: "It really is us! We are the church. If we want things to be different, we need to do something about it." Blaming the pastor, the director of Christian education, the deacons, the trustees, or whoever might be a possibility tends to diminish. "We are the ones to do something. What is it we are going to do?" Committed groups move in to take action as a team.

Creativity goes up because of the search for qualitative approaches and answers to address the group's concerns. This is true in the church.

When power and participation are confined to a few, those few are the ones who are expected to respond in creative ways and to arrive at innovative plans and solutions. When group members share in power and participation, the task belongs to them as well. They become involved in the search whether it has been tried there before, whether another congregation has tested it, or whether it seems to be something entirely new. They want a good fit. They would like their church to achieve its mission in more than "ho-hum" ways.

Recognition of Feelings

Effective leaders recognize that feelings are genuine and a central part of the whole person. They are willing to share their own feelings when it is appropriate. They encourage group members to share theirs. While they are not likely to dwell long on the feeling level unless the situation calls for it, neither do they ignore feelings assuming they are of little or no import.

These leaders give particular attention to dealing with negative feelings such as anger and hostility. They do not pretend that these feelings are irrelevant to what happens in a group. Perhaps experience has taught them that bottled-up negative feelings tend to grow and magnify. These confined feelings can interfere with each step the group tries to take. Soon the entire process of the group may bog down. Some members may choose to leave rather than stay in these stagnated relationships.

Negative feelings, differences, and conflict are generally little easier for leaders to deal with than for other group members. In some cases they may even be more difficult, but effective leaders are willing to work through the tough areas. They attempt to build a climate where group members come to realize that, although painful and hard, there is much to be learned from addressing these areas. Conflict can be an avenue to creativity if the group is willing to work step-by-step toward understanding, defining, and choosing ways to address the problem. Somehow effective leaders build confidence, model skills, and present a vision that the group has resources to face and handle conflict.

Many church congregations seem to have a particularly difficult time with negative feelings and conflict. Somehow the belief seems to exist that "if we are good Christians, these kinds of things shouldn't happen; therefore we won't let them happen. We will turn our heads the other way and pretend to be peaceful, happy, and full of good will." Of course, such a belief is not supported biblically. The Bible recognizes anger but sets forth such guidelines as to be angry for good causes and not to hold onto anger over a period of time. Conflict of various kinds is pervasive in the biblical books. Paul's letters to the early churches help us to gain perspective. Those churches were anything but conflict-free! Paul, from a distance, is attempting to help these little churches come to terms with their conflicts. One of the creative outcomes of the conflicts in the early churches is that we now have Paul's letters as part of our New Testament.

Flexibility

Effective leaders demonstrate a kind of flexibility which they incorporate into their ways of being leaders in the group. They are flexible at a number of levels. Let's consider two.

Robert Greenleaf believes that the church today is in desperate need of servant leaders who have a sense of the unknowable and who can do "contingency thinking."[3] The sense of the unknowable allows leaders to do the kind of thinking that moves beyond available, obvious facts to the uncharted and the unknown. Leaders need to develop the ability to use their intuitions and to believe in the process enough to use rather than lose their thoughts when the time is right and the need is there.

Leaders use contingency thinking when the unexpected happens and they have to act. Group members need to be confident that their leaders will not be so surprised or disarmed by the unusual that they paralyze or act randomly. Rather, the leaders will act promptly with a sensible response. Leaders need flexibility in their thinking.

Leaders also need to be flexible in the possession of power. They must sensitively determine when the situation is of such character that the most advantageous action for the group is for the leaders' power to operate, or when the situation is such that power is best shared among all the members equally. One reason leaders may tend to keep as much power as they can is that the preceding process requires great discernment and flexibility. It is not easy. There are no clear-cut lines.

Goal Formation

Finally, effective leaders are concerned about the goals of the group. They know that the goals toward which the group aspires are important. They realize that goals are necessary for group health. They also recognize that not just any goal will make that contribution. So they seek goals that will promote group health and vitality.

Goals that are clear and understood by all group members contribute to the health of the group. The job of the leaders becomes to clarify and to make sure that the group has reached an acceptable level of understanding as to what each goal means.

Goals must be within reach of the group. At least the group must make recognizable progress toward achieving the goals. At the same time, goals which are too easy carry no challenge. Leaders have to guide the group's goal-setting process so that the goals chosen carry a real challenge which has power to draw on the group's creativity and resources, but which goals are not entirely out of reach. The leader may have to initiate the process whereby the group clarifies ways the goals can actually be met.

In the church context, leaders have to scrutinize the goals as they are emerging to assess their theological integrity. "Anything we can do" is not an acceptable goal in the church. Those things which enhance God's kingdom and which continue Jesus' ministry of redemption and reconciliation should become our goals. Sometimes in the fervor of wanting to set attractive, appealing, or unique goals, a group may lose sight of the theological criteria to assess what they are doing and the direction they are setting. Leaders may be the ones to hold the group accountable.

In summary, there are key behaviors which are associated with being an effective leader. Five have been noted. Effective leaders work to establish a climate of trust, to communicate to all group members that they are important participants, to recognize that feelings are genuine and a central part of the whole person, to demonstrate a kind of flexibility, and, finally, to be concerned about the goals of the group.

It is noteworthy that all of these behaviors require followers who also care and work hard at being responsible members of the group. Quality leadership happens when all members of the group—leaders and followers—work together as a team. When leadership happens this way in the church, we experience something of what it means to be the body of Christ in action.

8
CHAPTER

Responding Supportively to Church Leadership

"Is anybody out there?"
"Does anybody care?"
"Please show us!"

Too often leaders feel that they are taken for granted in the church. "No one really cares much about what I do except when the job doesn't get done, then they care a lot. Not about me! About the fact that the job didn't get done!"

If the leaders feel a sense of nonsupport and a lack of caring, their followers may not only *feel*, they may *know* no one cares about them. "Nobody notices when I'm not there." "Oh, anyone can do what I do." "I'm just an add-on. It doesn't make any difference when I don't show up."

The above perceptions may not be accurate from the viewpoints of others who believe and feel that they do care about both leaders and followers. Church congregations do not have a hurtful agenda of putting people in leader positions and leaving them there to feel isolated and nonsupported; nor do they want to overlook the followers. Their intentions are good and quite in line with a solid theology of the church. Everyone counts; everyone has gifts and a place to serve in the body of Christ; everyone is important in making this church what it is. But their theology doesn't get implemented to any great extent when it comes to actual practice.

Part of the problem grows from the fact that support networks rarely develop and stay healthy in an automatic fashion. Just because persons believe that support is crucial does not mean that supportive ways of behaving will flow naturally.

We can learn a lesson from a marriage where a husband and a wife pledge to love, cherish, and honor each other for a lifetime. Their deep commitment and devotion at the time of the wedding is obvious. A decade later they may be in the pastor's office seeking counsel as to avenues they can take to save their painful, stressful relationship. They have come to an awareness that for ten years they have taken each other for granted. Now they have arrived at the point where they are not sure about love. They both feel ignored and misunderstood. They aren't sure whether it is worth the struggle to change; yet if they can't turn things around, they both want to be free from the continued hurt and pain of the relationship.

This couple at the time they were married would undoubtedly have professed intentions of support and understanding with regard to each other as they moved together into the future. They may have assumed for a period of time that support was actually happening. Maybe at first it did; but they did not work continually at being supportive in conscious ways. One day that nagging feeling that the other didn't really care began to surface. Over time it grew.

If this kind of dynamic operates in marriage where commitment is supposedly deeply binding and lifelong, is it so surprising that a similar dynamic operates in church life? The time period can be relatively short when church members, whether in leader or follower positions, begin to feel and believe that their involvements in leadership are not appreciated or supported.

We do not have to accept the dynamic as an inevitable negative process. There are purposeful ways to work at developing a strong, supportive, caring climate where people feel and know that they do count, that others do care and are grateful, that there is both general and specific support. Some congregations are doing a good job; others are doing some things well; some need to get started.

Research in volunteer organizations reveals that a key factor in determining whether volunteers continue to serve and feel good about their contributions is the extent to which they feel appreciated and supported. Congregations need to take this seriously and ask, "What can we do to be more effective in building support among our church members?"

Building a Supportive Climate

Being listened to is central to whether or not persons feel supported. It is a cherished gift when we sense that another person has chosen and genuinely wants to listen to our story. We respond to that kind of caring from the depths of our lives.

Listening processes in congregational life can be very inadequate. Let me draw from two personal life experiences as illustrations. They are selected from a number that could be used. Readers can likely supply their own life stories.

Our family had just arrived in the city so that Myron (my husband) and I could work on our doctoral degrees in graduate school. Our daughter was four; I was pregnant. Myron's mother was with us. There were many adjustments to make. We were worn and weary, having just moved from a demanding campus ministry position. An area pastor called on us in our partially moved-into home. He began telling us how delighted he was that we were in the area. He had long lists as to how our gifts and skills could be used in his church. We asked some tentative questions about that church contributing to our lives. We began to share with him something about our weariness and concerns about adjustment and overload. He continued to think of "opportunities" he had overlooked and added them to his ever-lengthening list. We quit talking; he eventually left. We did not join that church.

Another incident happened when our son was very ill. A woman called wanting me to provide major leadership at a regional conference. I mentioned to her that our son would likely be entering the hospital within the next month for extended therapy. "Oh, I'm sorry," she quickly moved on, saying, "We could, if it were absolutely necessary, squeeze your presentations into one day. It would interrupt our flow, but we *could* adjust if we had to." I tried once more to explain that our son's illness could be life-threatening. Again she urged me to accept her invitation because "your gifts are just what

84 DEVELOPING LEADERSHIP IN THE TEACHING CHURCH

we need. The entire planning team will be so disappointed if you say no." I told her I had to return to the care of our son. I could not continue to talk. My answer to her invitation was, "No, I am not available."

These are dramatic examples, but they happened. I have many memories of less consequential events which could have been used. I wanted to choose two that speak for themselves and which contrast with two others at the same life periods. The ones I just described left me feeling unheard, misunderstood, and definitely unsupported.

When listening processes operate well, the outcomes are very different. The following two illustrations tell their own story.

Another area pastor visited our home just after our move to attend graduate school. His style was very different. Two lay persons had called a week earlier. The pastor came later and began with a brief introduction to the church and its programs, but he then moved to asking us some gentle, conversational questions to discover who we were. He listened to our stories and observed, "You will be very busy. I'm not sure how you're going to do it all. I think you would find a supportive fellowship in our church." We joined that church. We somehow found time to be more active in its life than we ever anticipated. Over time, Myron and I both taught church school and participated in other ways. Myron's mother was active in the women's fellowship. Melody joined the children's choir; baby Tim was welcomed into the nursery. The doctoral robes Myron and I now wear at each seminary commencement were gifts from members of that congregation when we moved. They serve as reminders of the love, care, and support we experienced as part of them.

Another incident occurred during our son's illness. Months before he became sick I was committed to do a week's conference during the following summer. When I realized I would be involved in extended care for Tim's needs, I called the woman who had recruited me. She first voiced her disappointment, then she moved into asking questions about Tim's condition. She discovered the ambiguities and uncertainties our family was facing. There was so much we didn't know. "We would really like to have you at the conference. Are you willing to work on some contingency plans?" she asked me. She shared with me her thoughts about an alternate plan which they could implement if at the last minute I could not be at the conference. I agreed to explore it. The planning group did the work. The backup scheme was never used. I went to the conference. Our son was in the hospital and special arrangements were made to care for his needs. It was not easy, but throughout the week I felt much support. An adjustment was made in my schedule for the week so that I could complete the long-distance phone calls to the hospital at an appropriate time. I felt listened to. I felt loved and supported.

The last two illustrations purposely stand in stark contrast to the first two. All four are real events in my life. I hope that they communicate with some force the importance of listening and responding appropriately. A climate of support thrives on these ingredients.

Listening requires some skills, a level of desire and commitment, and a trustworthy climate. Perhaps the most formidable barrier to listening that we have to deal with in church life is time. Listening takes time. There is no adequate shortcut. It is one thing for a person to call and ask you to accept a responsibility and get your "Yes," "No," or "Let-me-think-about-it-and-call-you-back" response. It is quite another thing for the caller to move beyond your initial answer to listen to your feelings and concerns. It may be that you said yes but you're worried about doing a respectable job, given that you're feeling overloaded at work. You may have said no and now your guilt level is soaring. Perhaps you said, "I need time to think about it" and you're struggling with why it seems impossible for you to say no in a direct way.

If persons are to feel supported, we have to find time to listen to them from the beginning of the leadership process to the end. Perhaps instead of reporting back a simple answer to the nominating committee, the contact member might be responsible for describing some of the person's thoughts and feelings about that answer. Rather than just giving an announcement or a brief summary of facts related to a completed program, we could ask the person in charge, "How did it go for you?"

One congregation had a special service to recognize its charter members, most of whom were growing old enough to find church attendance problematic. The recognition service was memorable. It flowed beautifully with no noticeable flaws. Memories drew forth chuckles, smiles, frowns, and tears. It was a highlight occasion. At the next meeting of the general church board a number of positive comments were made. The chairperson suggested, "We need to have the secretary write a special letter to Mrs. deFries for chairing the service. She did a marvelous job. We need to tell her so." Everyone agreed. Just as the board was about to move to a new agenda item, a friend of Mrs. deFries commented, "Maybe someone ought to hand deliver the letter." A conspicuous silence begged her to elaborate. She went on. "I agree with everything we've said. The service was great. Everything turned out, but Marci deFries was a wreck. She was so worried about it. A lot of people backed out. She had trouble pinning people down. She was in bed for two days afterward with a migraine—or something. She told me that she hopes nobody asks her to do another thing in this church."

Mrs. deFries was recruited as a leader. No one on the board seemed to know much about her sad tale. Nobody had checked up. Everyone had expected her to plan an outstanding service. "She always does." The chairperson and the pastor agreed to take the letter. This board needed to spend some time developing ways to prevent a similar incident from happening again, if at all possible. Do you think they did?

In addition to listening, a supportive climate tends to develop when people are genuine, clear, and congruent in their communication with one another. We have already touched on this in the discussion of being trustworthy.

Being genuine, clear, and congruent means that we say what we mean, we clarify our meanings, we follow through on our promises, we have our words and our nonverbals together in one clear message. A few illustrations will highlight the challenge.

The board of Christian education in one church was concerned about securing new youth sponsors. The couple who had been doing a superb job had moved. The board had made several contacts with no success. One member was charged with phoning the next possible recruit. His phone call appeal went something like this: "We're having trouble finding somebody to sponsor the youth group. We know you're good with kids. We thought just maybe you'd do it. Everybody seems to think it's going to be so much work. Well, it isn't that bad. . . . We'll fill in for you if you have to be gone. . . . The parents are always willing to help if you ask. . . . "

Perhaps you can finish the appeal. You can also perceive how the recruiter was "softening the task." Sponsoring the youth group is an awesome responsibility. To do so takes much understanding, patience, time, and energy. It is not always easy to locate substitutes nor do substitutes necessarily have a positive experience so that they are willing to serve more than once. Parents are not always willing to help. You may find other ambiguities and fallacies in the presentation.

Another board was seeking teachers for a newly formed, rapidly growing young adult church school class. The couple they wanted to ask to team teach the class were busy people. Before asking them, the board members did some initial planning and contacting. When they made their appeal to the teaching couple, they presented these details: "We know you have gifts in team teaching. Our young adults need someone like you. We know you are busy. We understand that you have to be away sometimes. We have enlisted some others to work with you. The Lawrences will work with you and the class officers to do visiting in the homes and to plan social events. John Alexander and Sue Williams are willing to be substitutes when you cannot be there."

The differences between these two conversations with regard to genuineness, clarity, and congruity are dramatic. Perhaps you could imagine the nonverbal voice tones as you read them. Maybe you have had these kinds of contrasting experiences in your own pilgrimage in church life.

Persons need to be recruited to leader positions with openness and honesty. They need to receive support from the time they are recruited until they have finished and have had time to gain perspective on their leader experience.

If this kind of ongoing support is to happen, it has to be planned. It would happen only spasmodically, if at all, if it were left to chance. When support is present in consistent ways, it is because people have worked at it. There is no set way to show support. No one pattern provides an answer. Each congregation has to forge its own best way of being supportive. The following concrete suggestions may at least stimulate your thinking about your own congregation. They may serve as a springboard for you to create your own best ways.

Concrete Suggestions for Showing Support

In the initial stages when persons are being invited to accept a leadership challenge, it is important to be genuine and clear. The following questions raise issues and suggest possibilities.

Have your recruiters spent time on developing job descriptions for leaders and for followers? What is it that people are being asked to do? I remember the first time I received a job description for being a member of a group—not the leader. I knew what was expected of me. It was a simple list, but it was clear. It told me things such as how often we met and for what purpose, how much preparation was involved, whom to call if I couldn't attend. It helped me feel confident about the group and how I fit in.

Have recruiters considered the listening-time factor discussed earlier in this chapter? Do you know the thoughts and feelings that lie behind whatever response was given to a specific invitation to serve?

Have plans been made to orient the leaders to their positions? I was elected to serve as church clerk a number of years ago. I'd never been church clerk before. When I was asked to do it, the recruiter described the job as taking minutes at two-semiannual meetings. I was amazed when the outgoing clerk called and asked if we could schedule two hours at the church so she could show me everything and explain the job to me. The meeting lasted closer to three hours and I learned a lot. As we were leaving the church building, the outgoing clerk said, "I hope this helped. When I took the job six years ago, nobody told me anything. I had to figure it out by myself." I knew what she meant. I had accepted a position in the women's fellowship several years earlier. I'd found a box of "stuff" related to the job on my doorstep when I got home. I had never been sure what I was supposed to be doing with that position.

Do persons have a clear picture as to who will give help when they need it? If they have to locate people to work with them, are there any suggestions? I was asked to teach in a kindergarten Sunday church school class. The person who recruited me knew I would need a co-teacher. She gave me the names of three persons to contact, explaining to me that the board of Christian education had thought it would be best for me to select the person with whom I would most enjoy working. I was also given the name and phone number of the superintendent in case I had to be absent or if I had need for more help. There was an information sheet that told me how to order supplies through the person who purchased curriculum materials. There were also instructions for securing audiovisual equipment.

Does anyone write appreciation notes to the persons who have said yes? Are follow-up notes written to those who said no? It feels good to know that someone cares about responses, both positive and negative.

Are formal services of leadership commissioning and dedication planned? Do they ever highlight the important role of followers as well as leaders? (See Appendix 2 for some suggestions.)

The need for support does not end with the initial recruitment stages. When leadership is in progress, support is still a crucial variable. It can be offered in many ways.

Small group support commitments hold much promise. In one church two-person teams covenanted to study and pray together. They regularly made contact with each other. One of the outcomes was a feeling of caring and support. In another congregation a small group of several members committed themselves to pray for and support the Sunday church school. They were unable to teach on a regular basis themselves but they became a great resource for providing many other services. One member of the congregation commented to me. "Our Sunday church school experienced a renewal growing out of the concern of that group." Such groups could be organized and structured in many ways.

Highlights in worship, in newsletters, in bulletins, or on designated bulletin boards can feature various persons and the contributions they make in leadership. One church newsletter highlighted a junior high student who had mastered the skills of running all of the audiovisual equipment. When the reporter asked him what he would like to do next, he said, "Well, I'd like to learn how to fix the stuff and I want to teach some other kids how to run it. What if we need two things at once? I can't be in two places at the same time!" It was an inconspicuous job in many ways but a strategic one. It deserved to be recognized and affirmed.

I was impressed in one church that a bulletin board just outside the sanctuary had an attractive title: "Our Youth as Leaders." It carried

90 DEVELOPING LEADERSHIP IN THE TEACHING CHURCH

a beautiful picture display of church youth serving in many ways in the life of the church as well as in service to the community. An elementary child came by as I was looking at it. His grin at me caught my attention. When I looked at him, he pointed to two different pictures, "That's my brother. That's my sister." He didn't have to examine the board. He obviously knew where the pictures were. He had looked at it before. I asked him if he were in any of the pictures. He shook his head vigorously, "Nope. I was up there last time with the kids. I was in three pictures." He stood straight and tall as he explained it to me. The attractiveness of the display and my encounter with the child convinced me of the value of the Christian education bulletin board in that church. I learned that a new display was posted every two months, September through May. During the summer months the board was open for snapshots of various activities.

Committees and boards can set aside designated times for listening and "catching up" with the state of affairs with ongoing leadership involvements related to their work. These times can be informative as well as supportive.

Services designed to recognize and show appreciation for leadership can make concrete statements to leaders that we know you are there and we appreciate what you are doing. We have not put you in a leadership position, expected you to perform, and then forgotten you. (See Appendix 2 for suggestions.)

As leadership commitments come to a close, there is still a need for support. Plans need to be made for the smooth transfer of responsibility. Transitions to new opportunities for service need to be presented. Recognition for energies invested and gifts well used needs to happen at various levels. Services which recognize personal use of gifts can make significant statements to the persons who have served, as well as to other members of the congregation. The presentation of certificates can be a concrete way of expressing thanks to those who have served. (See Appendix 2 for suggestions.)

Opportunities also need to be given in smaller groups for closure among persons who have worked together. Often time for this can be a portion of the last scheduled meeting of the group or committee. It might involve a special event planned to highlight special memories, recognize gifts well used, and affirm stronger relationships which have been built. Sometimes persons leave responsibilities by simply "not coming anymore," and nothing is said about all that they have done to contribute to the life and ministry of the church. They may wonder if anyone was aware or cared about their contributions.

Leadership Training as Support

One specialized kind of support of persons in leadership positions is training which provides them opportunities for personal growth in the faith, as well as sharpened skills to do the job they are being asked to do. Leadership training is an important ministry of the church, but it can be fraught with issues and problems. The issue of life development and leadership training which needs to be addressed has been mentioned in chapter 4.. This discussion relates primarily to youth and adult leaders.

Trying to get church leaders to attend training events poses a challenge. Their lives are busy and time is at a premium. One pastor shared with a group, "When I first started in ministry thirty years ago, we used to hold four weeks of teacher-training sessions in the fall and four weeks of training for board members in the spring. We had good attendance every night—sometimes 100 percent. But not anymore. We don't even try to hold those kinds of meetings in the church I serve now. It would never work. We are lucky to find one day when even 75 percent can be there. Our board of Christian education really gets discouraged."

Another member of the group said a similar thing had happened in her church. "We try to get people to go to national and regional events, but that's hard, too. Everyone seems to be too busy."

"But I think our people need training as much or maybe even more than before," observed a third member of the group. "I think we've got to find new ways if the old ways won't work anymore."

Structures

Some congregations are searching for new structures to do leadership training. The apprenticeship model is being used where a new and less experienced person works alongside one with more experience. This approach is centuries old, but its revival today may be a workable approach in the modern context.

Another structure which some congregations have tried is to introduce a training component into regular meetings of boards and committees. Thirty to forty-five minutes are spent in learning together. (Appendix 1 of this book has outlines for groups studying this book chapter by chapter during meetings of a board or committee.) In some cases the focus has been primarily on group processes and skills; some churches have done more in terms of Bible study. One pastor reported, "I'm convinced that some of the best Bible study we're doing is by our board of deacons. It's great. We spend the first thirty minutes of our meetings in studying God's Word together. I used to do all of the teaching, but now some of the others are leading the session. At the end of the meeting we take fifteen minutes to pray together. We are all amazed at what is happening."

Another congregation set aside the business of the general church board for six weeks, except for absolute essentials. They took those six weeks and committed them to training in leadership dynamics and in-depth study of the Bible. At the end of the six weeks they moved into planning. "It made an unbelievable difference. It's incredible!"

Local church retreat models can be effective. An all-day retreat or an overnight can provide opportunities for intense training.

Many congregations will need to use several avenues for training their leadership, drawing on local, regional, denominational, and ecumenical resources. A package of approaches that touches the lives of the leaders in positive, change-producing ways may prove to be most effective in leadership training.

Content

In addition to structure, the content of leadership training is an important issue. Where should we begin? What should be included? Where should the emphasis be?

There is no one right answer to these questions. The best answers are those which fit the needs of the congregation. For some churches the most appropriate beginning point may be in study of the Bible, in exploration of the meaning of discipleship, and in experiences of group prayer together. Others may find that learning about leader/follower dynamics seems to be the most helpful launching point. It could be that a specialized focus, such as what it means to be a teacher or Bible study leader, could be a meaningful point to begin. There are some excellent leadership training programs available for local churches to use. There are helpful books which can be read. Selected lists of programs and books have been provided in Appendix 3.

Levels of Experience

Those who are responsible for leadership training need to be aware of levels of experience. If leaders have been through a training event, they don't want to have to repeat an identical one a year later. They need to move a step deeper this time or delve into another area altogether. One lay person lamented, "I've been coming to training events for years, but they seem like such a repeat. I'd really like to be challenged to grow. I keep hoping for something new." Another veteran of training events agreed with her. As I listened to their conversation, I realized that we need to hear and respond to this concern. Where do we go from initial training? What do advanced training experiences look like?

Leadership training is a crucial dimension of showing support to those involved in the leadership process. It must be well planned, strategically structured, and sensitively designed to meet the needs of the people involved. Less than quality events and experiences can seem more like a burden and an overload than a means of supportive undergirding. Our training opportunities must be done in qualitative ways.

Support of leadership is necessary from beginning to end so that leadership persons in your church can declare emphatically, "Somebody is out there supporting us. They show us they care in very concrete ways. They provide us with opportunities to learn and grow. Gone are the days when we wondered if anybody was out there, if anybody cared, and if anybody would ever show us."

A Final Challenge

Christians have been called to follow Jesus and, through him, to be reconciled to God. We are persons who have followed that call. We have become members of the body of Christ. We have been entrusted with continuing the ministry begun by Jesus. We have been empowered by the Holy Spirit. We are God's people.

When we think of ourselves in these terms, it is almost too much to believe. Full understanding lies beyond our capacities to comprehend. The complete reality is beyond us.

We do, however, see through the glass darkly. We experience something of our potential. We know we need to move beyond where we are.

We need the whole body of Christ to function to capacity. Our leadership dynamics must be optimal to assure that we are becoming all that we can be. We need leaders with vision and courage. We need followers with commitment and persistence. We need each member of the body contributing the gifts each has been given by the Spirit.

It is a great challenge to live as God's people as we approach the twenty-first century. Adequate answers for today's tasks may provide only partial answers for tomorrow's. The day after that may require new insights altogether.

Whenever we serve as leaders or as followers, we must think of our contributions as essential to the well-being of the church and its mission. The challenge to be God's people, the body of Christ, the new humanity, the fellowship of believers, the household of God, belongs to us. We are God's instruments in today's world. The challenge is ours. We are called to leadership!

APPENDIX 1

Brief Session Outlines for a Group Studying This Book

The following session outlines related to each chapter are brief. Each contains ideas for a three-phase session. Two possibilities are given, either of which might be used to get group members involved. Four or five ideas are suggested for exploring the content of the chapter. Some of them emphasize application of the ideas to your study group or to the congregation. Finally, two suggestions are made for reaching closure. Because the outlines are brief, the facilitator will have to give considerable thought to selection of specific teaching activities and to detailed planning for a particular group. Some of the suggestions may be used for personal reflection and study by the individual reader.

Chapter 1: Looking at Church Leadership

Getting Involved: (1) Brainstorm a list of ways that leaders are "key people" in your congregation. (2) Identify some of the leaders' dreams in the history of your church which have helped shape who your church is today.

Exploring the Chapter: (1) Imagine you are the core leaders who do not want to settle for mediocre quality. Formulate a "vision list"

97

of things you can do better to be what God intends for your church. Discuss how these things might become a reality. (2) Do a leader analysis of your church. (If your church is large, you may want to select one or two boards for consideration.) Note the formal and informal leaders. Discuss how these persons help to move the church (or board) toward its goals. (3) Make a list of leadership events that people can recall happening in the life of your church where the interaction among leaders and followers really counted. (4) Supply the specific details from incidents in the life of your church when quality leadership worked and when it seemed to stumble. Analyze what went right and what could have been improved.

Reaching Some Closure: (1) Write cards telling how each one senses the call to leadership in the life of the church. Share the cards. (2) Ask each group member to formulate a sentence prayer related to one of the images of the church.

Chapter 2: Biblical Touchstones for Church Leadership

Getting Involved: (1) Have each member react to the following scale: "If we were to have our church's principles of leadership based on a solid biblical/theological foundation, we would have to. . . . "

begin from zero
do some work
refine what we have

(2) Ask group members to describe a biblical touchstone they have used in their own lives.

Exploring the Chapter: (1) Summarize each of the five touchstones. Add other insights and illustrations which could have been included in the discussion. (2) List other touchstones which could be useful. (3) Discuss God's call to leadership. Share in what senses, if at all, persons in the group feel called by God as members of the church. (4) If Paul were to write a letter to your church about problems you face in being the body of Christ, what would he include? Make a list.

Reaching Some Closure: (1) Spend some time in silent reflection and meditation. (2) Sing "Spirit of the Living God."

Chapter 3: Spiritual Gifts and Church Leadership

Getting Involved: (1) Ask group members to share their reactions to "turning the clock back" through imagination. (2) Have group members give their own ideas as to what a spiritual gift is.

Exploring the Chapter: (1) Work through each of the four Scripture passages, listing primary ideas and insights about spiritual gifts. (2) Make a spiritual gifts assessment list of the gifts present in the group. Persons can give their own or others can contribute their observations. (3) Discuss ways in which spiritual gifts may be abused in your congregation. You may add to the list in the chapter. (4) Describe how your church cultivates spiritual gifts of its members. What more could you do?

Reaching Some Closure: (1) Pray personally for stewardship of spiritual gifts. (2) Share a commitment for using one's gifts to build up your group.

Chapter 4: Lifelong Pilgrims in Church Leadership

Getting Involved: (1) Ask several group members to share an incident from their childhood which taught them something about leading or following. (2) Call for reactions to the pastor's statement that "babies are dictators."

Exploring the Chapter: (1) Ask each one to make a leadership time line on newsprint. Note at least one significant event at each life stage. These can be shared in small groups or with the entire group. (2) List ways your church is helping to cultivate leadership potential at each life stage. (3) Brainstorm approaches your church could undertake to address better the nurturing of leadership throughout the whole life pilgrimage. (4) Analyze how the church helped develop the leadership potential of the members of the group.

Reaching Some Closure: (1) Request that class members identify a leadership challenge to which they need to give particular attention at this life stage. (2) Make commitments to become involved in nurturing the leadership capacity of others.

Chapter 5: Creating a Climate for Church Leadership Commitment

Getting Involved: (1) Compare your congregation with Church Alive and Church Adrift. (2) Allow a time for sharing by group members about other churches which seem to be like Church Alive or Church Adrift.

Exploring the Chapter: (1) List the four factors of high cohesion, mutual support, efficiency, and adaptability. Make an analysis of how well your church performs on each one. Suggest ideas for improvement. (2) Work in three small groups to arrive at a projection list showing how well your congregation does and how you can improve the dynamics of the sense of the Holy Spirit, a vital small group ministry, and a core of committed leaders. (3) Ask group members to share the barriers in their own lives which cause them to struggle with invitations to leadership. Add their suggestions to those discussed in the book. (4) Discuss how the four levels of relationships work out in your own lives and leadership involvements. This could be done in four small subgroups.

Reaching Some Closure: (1) Write a group covenant containing concrete things this group of persons can do to increase vitality in your church. (2) Pray for renewed vitality of the Spirit's presence in your midst.

Chapter 6: Church Leadership in Action

Getting Involved: (1) Use the group you are in and trace how leadership has developed. How did group members go about defining themselves? (2) Allow time for persons to share what it was like when they emerged as leaders but group members seemed to forget that they were members of the team.

Exploring the Chapter: (1) Ask members to assess their own leader styles. If you want to use a simple instrument, see the book *Joining Together* (note 2, chapter 6). Other books already in your church library may have instruments. You can simply use text materials and have persons write out their own profiles, using the discussion in the text. (2) Conduct an analysis of the needs of your group and how the leadership patterns of the group have addressed those needs. (3) Identify two or three boards/committees in your church which seem to require something different in terms of leadership patterns. List some factors which seem to contribute to those differences. (4) Spend some time reflecting on the importance of the questions that end the chapter. These additional issues could be raised: What should you do if you make a mistake and can't handle a leadership situation? Does God call us to situations we can't handle?

Reaching Some Closure: (1) Ask members to share one or two positive things about their leader styles. If time permits, set a growth goal leading toward more flexibility. (2) Share ways in which members are willing to commit themselves to improving or to maintaining a healthy leadership balance in your church.

Chapter 7: Keys to Effective Church Leadership

Getting Involved: (1) After asking group members to think about an outstanding leader or two they have known, brainstorm a list of traits that describe the leaders. Discuss the results in light of the leaders they had in mind. What can be learned? Do all the leaders have all of the traits? (2) Have group members state whether they agree or disagree with the following statement: "Leaders are really much more the key to group life than followers." Discuss their reasons.

Exploring the Chapter: (1) Explore how situations have made a difference in how effective leaders are by discussing the experiences of the group members—as leaders and/or as followers. (2) Use the five key leadership behaviors as a basis for group members to assess their strengths and to identify areas where they need to grow as leaders. (3) Draw on members' life experiences to show how increased participation leads to increased commitment and creativity. Apply the insights to your church. (4) To add to the two illustrations in the text, brainstorm a more complete list of areas where leaders need to be flexible.

Reaching Some Closure: (1) Sing the hymn "Renew Thy Church" or a similar hymn. (2) Using the personal assessments made by group members related to the five key leader behaviors, pray for one another's growth in service and ministry.

Chapter 8: Responding Supportively to Church Leadership

Getting Involved: (1) Ask persons to assess whether they believe the leaders in your church feel very little support or a great deal of support. Encourage them to give reasons for their assessments. (2) Ask some members of the group to share examples from their

102 DEVELOPING LEADERSHIP IN THE TEACHING CHURCH

past experience where feeling supported has caused them to "hang in." Explore how the support was shown in concrete ways.

Exploring the Chapter: (1) Spend time analyzing and contrasting the four examples from the author's life on being listened to. Share illustrations from group members' life experiences. (2) Make a list of persons in your congregation who need to be listened to. Begin with your own stories. Discuss how time for listening can be made available. (3) Poll the group as to how well they think your church succeeds in being genuine, clear, and congruent with one another. (4) Evaluate the effectiveness of the leadership training opportunities available to members of your congregation. What still needs to be done? (5) Begin a list of concrete things your church can do to make the support of its leadership more concrete and more effective.

Reaching Some Closure: (1) Pray for the person to your left. (2) Make a commitment to support another church member and share your commitment with the group and with that person.

2
APPENDIX

Suggestions for Planning Leadership Dedication and Recognition Services

The following resources contain skeleton suggestions for brief services of dedication and recognition for church leadership. The suggestions may be selected to take place within a larger service of worship or they can be expanded to become an entire service, with leadership among God's people as its focus. It is hoped that the ideas contained here become germinal seeds for you to do your own creative planning related to the specific needs of your congregation.

Calls to Worship

(A) *Leader:* God created persons to walk in covenant with God and with one another. In the beginning God called Adam and Eve to be in covenant relationship. Today the same God calls us. Come, let us worship our God together.

(B) *Leader:* There are different gifts in every life.
People: But it is the same Spirit who gives them.

Leader: There are different ways of serving God with our gifts.
People: But it is the same Lord who is served.
Leader: God works through different individuals in different ways.
People: But it is the same God whose purposes are achieved through them all.
Leader: Together we are the people of God.
People: Together we are the body of Christ.
All: We come as a called people to celebrate God's work among us. Let us worship together.
(C) *All:* God has called us to a great task. God's mission for us is to be Good News people in the whole earth. Come let us worship, that we might be renewed and strengthened for service.

Possible Scriptures

Old Testament: Deuteronomy 30:9-20; Joshua 24:14-18; 1 Samuel 3:1-10; Psalm 19; Psalm 23; Psalm 24; Psalm 63:1-4; Psalm 95:1-7; Psalm 121; Isaiah 6:1-8.

New Testament: Matthew 16:21-27; Mark 1:9-20; Luke 5:1-11; John 14:25-31; John 15:12-27; Romans 12:1-13; 1 Corinthians 12:1-26; Colossians 3:1-17; 1 Timothy 2:1-6; 1 Peter 2:9-10.

A Unison Prayer of Confession

O God, you have been Giver of life to us. You have given us breath for living each day. You have given us talents and abilities which make us unique persons. You have shown us through Jesus our Lord how life should be lived in obedience to your will. You have revealed your ways in Scripture. We know all of this and yet so often we turn from you to our own sinful choices, which result in alienation and brokenness. We rely primarily on our own wisdom and strength. We ignore our gifts or use them for our own personal enhancement. Forgive us. Fill us anew with your Spirit. Call us again to service in your name that we might be faithful stewards of life. In the name of Jesus, who was obedient to death, we pray. Amen.

Words of Assurance

God's presence is sure; God's call is certain. Jesus said that he would be with us always and even until the earth shall end. We can open our hearts, refresh our minds, lift up our heads and be renewed.

Litanies of Dedication and Recognition

(A) *Pastor:* God has given spiritual gifts to each Christian to be used to build up the church that we might be renewed and strengthened as the body of Christ.

Leaders: We thank you, O Lord, for the spiritual gifts you have given each of us.

Pastor: Our gifts are to be used in mission and service that the whole world might be filled with the Good News of Jesus Christ.

Leaders: We thank you, O Lord, for opportunities to serve in your name.

Pastor: Through the ages God has opened doors for persons to move into positions of faithful leadership. God has called all the people together to be who they are supposed to be as God's people. God continues to call persons today.

Leaders: We thank you, O Lord, for your call to us to leadership positions.

People: We thank you, O Lord, for your call to us to support our leaders and to be faithful stewards of our own gifts.

Pastor: God has promised to be with us. That promise is sure. We can live with confidence that God's love is steadfast; God's faithfulness is enduring.

All: Thank you, O Lord, for your love and faithfulness to us. Help us to be your faithful followers.

(B) *Pastor:* We have tried to be faithful in using our gifts in building up the body of Christ in the places where we have served.

Leaders: O Lord, we thank you for opportunities to build up the body of Christ.

Pastor: We have tried to be faithful in using our gifts in preparing ourselves and others for ministry and service in your name.

Leaders: O Lord, we thank you for opportunities for ministry and service.

Pastor: Sometimes some of us have felt that our serving has been effective and productive. We have seen an impact resulting from our being faithful followers.

Leaders: O Lord, we thank you for the victories in leadership.

Pastor: Other times some of us have felt discouraged and

defeated as if our efforts have achieved so little and in some cases been misunderstood. We have felt unsupported and alone.

Leaders: O Lord, we thank you for your abiding presence in times of discouragement and defeat.

Pastor: We would wait patiently to be renewed, that again we might go forth to do your service like the powerful eagles that mount and fly above the earth. Some of us will lead while others will follow, but all of us would join together recognizing we are your people, the body of Christ.

All: O Lord, we thank you that we are your people. We thank you for all of the members of the body of Christ. We thank you for one another.

Possibilities for Dedicating Entering Leaders

You might want to do any of the following: present each leader individually, name a prayer support person for each leader, have the pastor or chairpersons welcome the new leaders, provide opportunities for new leaders to give brief testimonies or ask one new leader to share more in depth on behalf of all.

Possibilities for Recognizing Ongoing or Retiring Leaders

You might want to do any of the following: present individual certificates recognizing service, have selected persons share how these leaders have had an impact on their lives, use slides (taken over time) to show these leaders in service, have a formal presentation which describes how these leaders have contributed to the life of the church, provide opportunities for leaders to share their stories.

Other parts of the service should be developed with the particular congregation and its needs in mind. The service should be planned to help people come into the presence of God and to go out renewed for ministry.

3
APPENDIX

Resources for Training and Reading

Resources for Training

Leader Development Resource. This system was developed by the Methodists to guide churches in planning what leaders are needed, how to locate potential leaders, how to enlist and place leaders, as well as how to prepare and support them. Available from Local Church Education, Board of Discipleship of the United Methodist Church, Service Dept., P.O. Box 871, Nashville, TN 37202.

The Ministry of Volunteers: A Guidebook for Churches. This is a comprehensive program which includes nine components including identifying, recruiting, training, and supporting volunteers. Consists of seven booklets which may be ordered as the complete guidebook or separately. Developed by the Office for Church Life and Leadership, United Church of Christ. Available from Church Leadership Resources, P.O. Box 179, St. Louis, MO 63166.

Training Volunteer Leaders. This program was developed by the YMCA. It is aimed more broadly than the church volunteer program, but it contains excellent suggestions. It is particularly strong in group process. Available from Research and Development Division, National Council of YMCA, 291 Broadway, New York, NY 10007.

Vision for Leadership. A flexible eighteen-workshop design for local churches, including three foundation, five role, and ten skill workshops. Strong on training boards and committees in the church as well as providing a background for leadership. Developed by the Division of Church Education, Educational Ministries, American Baptist Churches, USA. Available from Judson Book Store, Valley Forge, PA 19482-0851.

Resources for Further Reading

Byrne, H. W. *Improving Church Education.* Birmingham: Religious Education Press, Inc., 1979.

Greenleaf, Robert K. *Servant Leadership.* New York: Paulist Press, 1977.

Greenleaf, Robert K. *The Servant as Religious Leader.* Peterborough, N.H.: Windy Row Press, 1983.

Heusser, D-B. *Helping Church Workers Succeed: The Enlistment and Support of Volunteers.* Valley Forge: Judson Press, 1980.

Huber, Evelyn. *Enlist, Train, Support Church Leaders.* Valley Forge: Judson Press, 1975.

Johnson, Douglas W. *The Care and Feeding of Volunteers.* Nashville: Abingdon Press, 1978.

Lindgren, Alvin J. and Shawchuck, Norman. *Let My People Go: Empowering Laity for Ministry.* Nashville: Abingdon Press, 1980.

McDonough, Reginald M. *Working with Volunteer Leaders in the Church.* Nashville: Broadman Press, 1976.

Miller, Paul M. *Leading the Family of God.* Scottdale, Pa.: Herald Press, 1981.

Rusbuldt, Richard E. *Basic Leader Skills: Handbook for Church Leaders.* Valley Forge: Judson Press, 1981.

Shawchuck, Norman. *How to Be a More Effective Church Leader.* Indianapolis: Spiritual Growth Resources, 1981.

Shawchuck, Norman, *What It Means to Be a Church Leader.* Indianapolis: Spiritual Growth Resources, 1984.

Turner, Nathan W. *Effective Leadership in Small Groups.* Valley Forge: Judson Press, 1977.

Wagner, C. Peter. *Your Spiritual Gifts Can Help Your Church Grow.* Ventura, Calif.: Regal Books, 1979.

Walrath, Douglas A. *Leading Churches Through Change.* Nashville: Abingdon Press, 1979.

Wilson, Marlene. *How to Mobilize Church Volunteers.* Minneapolis: Augsburg Publishing House, 1983.

Notes

Chapter 1
[1] Martin Buber, *I and Thou* (Edinburgh: Clark, 1937).

Chapter 2
[1] Three recent books which are valuable in improving biblical study and interpretation skills are David L. Bartlett, *The Shape of Scriptural Authority* (Philadelphia: Fortress Press, 1983); Gordon Fee and Douglas Stuart, *How to Read the Bible for All It's Worth* (Grand Rapids: The Zondervan Corp., 1981); and William D. Thompson, *Preaching Biblically: Exegesis and Interpretation* (Nashville: Abingdon Press, 1981).

Chapter 3
[1] *Discover Your Gifts* (Grand Rapids: Christian Reformed Home Missions, third revised edition, 1983). Available from Christian Reformed Home Missions, 2850 Kalamazoo Avenue, S.E., Grand Rapids, MI 49560.

Chapter 5
[1] Ronald J. Webb, "Organizational Effectiveness and the Voluntary Organization" in *Academy of Management Journal* (Volume 17, 1974), pp. 663-667.
[2] Ernest G. Bormann and Nancy C. Bormann, *Effective Committees and Groups in the Church* (Minneapolis: Augsburg Publishing House, 1973), pp. 32-34.
[3] See Aaron Levenstein, *Why People Work* (New York: Crowell-Collier Press, 1962).

Chapter 6
[1] For a technical discussion, see B. Aubrey Fisher, *Small Group Decision Making* (New York: McGraw Hill, Inc., 1974).

112 DEVELOPING LEADERSHIP IN THE TEACHING CHURCH

[2] For more detailed discussions, see the following books: Jay Hall, *The Competence Process* (Woodlands, Texas: Teleometrics, International, Inc., 1980); David W. Johnson and Frank P. Johnson, *Joining Together* (Englewood Cliffs: Prentice-Hall, second edition, 1982); and Ernest Stech, *Leadership Communication* (Chicago: Nelson-Hall Publishers, 1983).

[3] See two books by Robert K. Greenleaf, *Servant Leadership* (New York: Paulist Press, 1977) and *The Teacher as Servant* (New York: Paulist Press, 1979).

Chapter 7

[1] See Bobby R. Patton and Kim Giffin, *Interpersonal Communication in Action* (New York: Harper and Row Publishers, Inc., second edition, 1977).

[2] Jay Hall, *The Competence Process*, p. 68.

[3] Robert Greenleaf, *The Servant as Religious Leader* (Peterborough, N.H.: Windy Row Press), pp. 16-17.